DEWEY AND RUSSELL
AN EXCHANGE

DEWEY AND RUSSELL
AN EXCHANGE

edited by Samuel Meyer

Philosophical Library
New York

Library of Congress Cataloging in Publication Data
Main entry under title:

Dewey and Russell--an exchange.

Bibliography: p.
1. Dewey, John, 1859-1952.   2. Russell, Bertrand,
1872-1970.   I. Meyer, Samuel.
B945.D44P49   1985   191   84-14886
ISBN 0-8022-2406-7

In honor of my parents, Minnie and Louis,
whose vision of freedom and culture
is a permanent heritage.

Contents

Acknowledgments

The author wishes gratefully to acknowledge permission to quote from the following sources:

The Basic Writings of Bertrand Russell, edited by Robert Egner and Lester E. Denonn. Copyright © 1961 by Allen & Unwin. Reprinted by permission of Pocket Books, a Simon and Schuster division of Gulf & Western Corporation.

A Common Faith, by John Dewey. New Haven: Yale University Press, 1934.

Contemporary American Philosophy: Personal Statements, George Plimpton Adams and William Pepperrell Montague, Editors. First published 1930; reissued, New York: Russell & Russell, 1962. London: George Allen & Unwin (Publishers) Ltd.

Inquiry into Meaning and Truth, by Bertrand Russell. New

Editor's Preface

I

Dewey and Russell are undoubtedly the two outstanding figures in Twentieth Century philosophy. While their personal contacts were cordial, to the extent of Dewey defending Russell in a law suit, helping to get him a job, and writing his last will and testament on his presumed deathbed in a Peking hospital (lawyer, doctor, confessor), their public encounters were bruising and abrasive affairs. While composing a reply to one of Russell's structures for *The Journal of Philosophy*, Dewey remarked, "You know, he gets me sore."[1]

Despite the public encounters and the private understandings, no serious attempt by either was made to get to the heart of the other's opposing arguments.

Russell's early investigations into mathematics had been challenged by the revolution of Planck's quantum and Einstein's relativity discoveries. He moved to meet this challenge in his work with Whitehead in *Principia Mathematica*. In philosophy he was again challenged by the revolutionary pragmatism of William James on the traditional notions of "truth" and the distinction of subject and object as fundamental.

"For my part, I am convinced that James was right on this matter .... I had thought otherwise until he, and those who agreed with him, persuaded me of the truth of his doctrine."[2] However much he may have been persuaded of the "truth of his doctrine," he could never bring himself to accept the consequences which this "truth" might entail. He thus found in Dewey a handy foil for his fundamental dissatisfaction with the doctrines of pragmatism or instrumentalism. This no doubt provided a greater satisfaction than making a serious effort to grasp Dewey's theory of knowledge. Surely it is not accidental that Russell relates: "In prison, I wrote first a polemical criticism of Dewey and then the Introduction to Mathematical Philosophy."

Russell's logic has a curiously Leibnitzean flavor. If nature is rational, it will correspond to the laws of mathematics. The underlying presupposition is a world of facts and a world of mathematical logic which correspond as mirror images. Atomic facts are reflected by atomic propositions.

"The justification of logical atomism—you can get down in theory, if not in practice, to ultimate simples, out of which the world is built, and that those simples have a kind of reality not belonging to anything else. The only other sort of object you come across in the world is what we call *facts* and facts are the sort of things that are asserted or denied by propositions, and are not properly entities at all."[3]

How and why an atomic proposition corresponds to an atomic fact is not indicated, but it is hoped that structural identity could be accomplished by a correspondence theory of truth and the ideal language of mathematical logic. Thus there is a correspondence between mathematical logic and the structure of the world. And this is precisely the dualistic, pre-established harmony most likely to draw Dewey's fire.

"It is impossible to force Mr. Bertrand Russell into any one of the pigeonholes of the cabinet of conventional philosophic schools. But moral, or philosophical, motivation is obvious in his metaphysics when he says that mathematics takes us 'into the region of absolute necessity, to which not only the actual world but every possible world must conform.' "[4]

In the same essay Dewey notes that: "A world that was all necessity would not be a world of necessity; it would just be. For in its being nothing would be necessary for anything else."[5]

As for the Russell-Whitehead magnum opus *Principia Mathematica*, in which the attempt is made to derive pure mathematics from logical concepts, Dewey has no scholarly comment on its subject matter or the techniques involved in this effort. He does, however, post a general danger sign in "doubting the existence of a faculty of pure reason independent of any and all experience, a faculty gifted with the power of infallible intuition."[6] Further, the meaning or force of universal propositions about logical forms, like mathematical axioms, is determined and tested by what follows from their operative use.

While Russell presents the case for classic analytic rationalism Dewey proposes improvisation to fashion tools hard and sharp with a cutting edge for solving each problem with its unique temporal circumstances as required. "*Moral* goods and ends exist only when something has to be done.... This ill is just the specific ill that it is. It is never an exact duplicate of anything else. Consequently the good of the situation has to be discovered, projected and attained on the basis of the exact defect to be rectified.... Classification *suggests* possible traits to be on the lookout for in studying a particular case.... They are tools of insight; their value is promoting an individualized response in the individual situation."[7] "And the pragmatic import of the

logic of individualized situations, each having its own irre-
placeable good and principle, is to transfer the attention of
theory from preoccupation with general conceptions to the
problem of developing effective methods of inquiry."[8] "If the
need and deficiencies of a specific situation indicate improvement of health as the end and good, then for that situation
health is the ultimate and supreme good. It is no means to
something else. It is a final and intrinsic value."[9]

Russell's search was for a system in which the real could be
mirrored by irreducible definitions, while for Dewey, logic was
an instrument for discovery arising out of the existing culture
dealing with the means employed to settle an indeterminate
situation. The question as to whether these two aspects of
logical theory, the demonstrative elements of *a priori* reasoning and the empirical scientific method, may be reconciled, the
possible and contingent with the rational and certain, remains.

II

To the generation that has grown to maturity since World
War II the most pertinent criticism both philosophers would
face today lies in their nineteenth century liberal optimism and
their lack of the sense of tragic vision. This critique is perhaps
most forcibly expressed in the philosophy of existentialism.

It is somewhat difficult to speak of man's innate goodness or
the generous impulses lying within our own breasts after
Auschwitz and Hiroshima. Indeed it becomes apparent that
the problem of material scarcity will not allow all men to
co-exist. We are rather a flesh-eating species whose aim is the
selective destruction of man. Each sovereignty will choose its
expendibles, not merely in war but as a matter of national
policy. Not even the glory of Kant's imperative comes to our
aid. We must question in what sense man is a free moral agent
and in what sense he is material subject to the same law of

causality as any other material of nature. Since as decent people we banish these stubborn ideas, we must unconsciously designate outgroups as sub-men in order that our digestive process may continue undisturbed.

This precisely is the "indeterminate situation" which, in Dewey's logic, calls for inquiry. The situation itself is immediately experienced in direct occurrence, and the observation of the material involved is "mediating in the temporal continuum constituting life experience." But in what sense can we reach a conclusion?

The *Timaeus* of Plato, in accounting for the creation of the world by Reason, had to introduce the element of force or necessity that lies at the heart of things. This force, or fate, is then channeled but not wholly conquered by Reason. The civilized world is based on this faith of the power of persuasion over irrational force. Yet the irrational is so plainly visible in our conduct as individuals and as states.

Spinoza believed in the possibility of attaining freedom from the irrational by the very act of understanding it. Dewey has pointed out that "the only form of enduring social organization that is now possible is one in which the new forces of productivity are cooperatively controlled and used in the interest of the effective liberty and the cultural development of the individuals that constitute society." Russell calls for maximizing production and keeping a stable population through birth control. There are no truth claims here, but evaluations and danger signs.

While Plato affirmed all possibilities on to infinity, he based this great chain on the so-called principle of plenitude, a notion that has aroused considerable scepticism. In our own times the nightmare of Malthus can be empirically observed. With the realization that basic needs are related to limited resources and that there is simply not enough to go around, entirely new and unprecedented problems arise. Man becomes a threat to himself if coexistence is no longer possible.

If we are no longer able to control our choice the only question to be answered is: Who shall be the victim. This question at once abolishes moral judgment and individual responsibility. It thrusts upon us the totalitarian ethic of nihilism.

The answer of the existentialist is a quantum leap into faith. He abandons all relationships except an existing individual. The only reality is the actuality of one's own being. Knowledge of the external world is merely a possibility but the existing individual is his own ethical reality. The contents of this ethical reality are whatever expresses his ultimate concern. It is difficult to imagine what this test would exclude, if it would exclude anything. Heidegger, the existentialist philosopher, hailed the rise of Hitler and urged the German universities to cooperate in the Nazi cause. Sartre was a Communist devoted to the possibility of a Marxian state minus Stalinism. Teilhard de Chardin embraced both forms of totalitarianism, including the deployment of the atomic bomb, as an evolutionary step to the goal of élitism.

It may be protested that existentialism has developed no political philosophy, and if indeed this is the case, what has been omitted is far more valuable than anything an acute observer might decide that it retains. Kierkegaard makes no pretense. Truth (as usual) must be abandoned to make room for faith. "The conclusions of passion are the only reliable ones. Reason is a whore."

But passions can not constitute a religion. If Kierkegaard is correct a dog would be man's exemplar, for there is no doubt that a hound's passions are as intense as, if less varied than, his master's, and all problems arising from principles of law, morality, politics and ethics can be obliterated.

If the existentialists were to bring one tenth of the energy they use to depict man's despair and desperate condition to meeting the problems of evil and scarcity that arise in the natural world, not only would we be closer to the solutions we so urgently require, but they would be free of most of the symptoms of nausea and vertigo they complain of. Through rifts in the clouds of pessimism careful observers can discern the beginnings of a new world science which is transforming every aspect of human nature. Existentialism, which is the direct heir of what has been called the "Counter-Enlightenment," is the regressive form of obscurantism that resists and retards the methods and goals of science.

It is evident that we are entering a new era. Since the first atom was smashed in the service of warfare, we have entered the Space Age, and perhaps even more important, the age of computer communication. This marks the third great advance in the possibility of civilization. The first was the discovery of Agriculture freeing man from the hunt and leading to the great river cultures. The second was the scientific and industrial revolution which freed man's energy for the accumulation of wealth and knowledge. The computer now promises the liberation of human thought for inquiry and creativity. The rapidity and scope of its progress are beyond description. Revolutions in genetics, biology and molecular structure are announced in our daily newspaper. A general convergence of all science is a genuine possibility. Dewey defined philosophy as a critique of critiques. What is needed now is a critique, or better, a science of sciences by which we can intelligently plan the present and control the future.

This science must exist in transmission as well as in communication. It is in communication and transmission that we can possess knowledge in common. Without this possession of shared activity we are hardly better off than a horse, who, as Dewey noted, does not really share in the social use to which his action is put. It is suggested that the great resources of the future will be not in minerals and oil but in scientific education and democracy, not merely as a parliamentary form of government, but as a way of life. In a few decades, with any sort of international conciliation, the wasting assets of petroleum and minerals will be replaced by nuclear, solar, and thermal energy. The race for survival will be replaced by the controlled planning of cosmic energy.

The impact of these technological advances on our society is already profound. Data banks on individuals and groups exist in federal agencies such as the C.I.A., the Pentagon, and the F.B.I., as well as in various private credit and banking services. The notion of privacy and individuality is already somewhat naive and archaic. The use of this far-reaching power in the hands of unprincipled executives can easily lead to a police state and a sublimated reign of terror. Forthright discussion and the utmost diligence in the protection of freedom is urgently and plainly required.

Our basic question is how far we shall allow the state to direct and control the physical and mental activities of individuals in their daily lives and their various associations. We already have suffered more grievances than those which inspired the colonies to revolt against King George. To Justice Holmes, wiretapping was "dirty business." "I think it less evil that some criminal should escape than that the government should play an ignoble part."[10] Perhaps the definitive structure of the issue was framed by Brandeis:

> The makers of our Constitution undertook to secure conditions favorable to the pursuit of happiness. They recognized the significance of man's spiritual nature, of his feelings and of his intellect. They knew that only a part of the pain, pleasure and satisfactions of life is to be found in material things. They sought to protect Americans in their beliefs, their thoughts, their emotions and their sensations. They conferred, as against the Government, the right to be let alone—the most comprehensive of rights and the right most valued by civilized men. To protect that right, every unjustifiable intrusion by the Government upon the privacy of the individual, whatever the means employed, must be deemed a violation of the Fourth Amendment. And the use, as evidence in a criminal proceeding, of facts

ascertained by such intrusion must be deemed a violation of the Fifth.[11]

It should be noted that these words form part of a *dissenting* opinion. After a thirty-three-year lapse the Brandeis doctrine became ruling law in 1961 when it was decided that illegally obtained evidence can no longer be admitted in any court in the United States, Federal or state.[12]

Our tireless bureaucrats are seldom discomforted by Supreme Court edicts. Why present evidence in court? They simply collect all available data and tapes and store them as evidence for inter-bureau use. What was once bluntly identified as "dirty business" is simply designated a "character profile" for such use as may best suit the exigencies of the moment. It is a matter of vital concern when any person's existence may, at the whim of any remote official, become a nightmare of frustration and chagrin. Since there are no rules of the sheer accumulation of these mountains of intimate details, for public as well as private agencies, I propose that the cumulative data of all such depositories, with the exception of the Bureau of Vital Statistics and ship registries, be completely destroyed every five years accompanied by a national celebration. This would give a sporting sabbatical start for every citizen and perhaps relieve us of the threat of a creeping police state.

III

Philosophy is a vision of the future. A philosopher reports this vision and the means of its attainment. Like art and religion it prepares us for problems that may not as yet have come to pass but which we will have to face. These include not only the intelligent adaptation of our institutions to the new scientific age, but the preservation of moral values and the enhancement of individual personality.

The truth values of the reflective thought of both Dewey and

Russell lie in the fact that these are the very problems that have been the keystone of their own respective philosophies. A signpost, however, whether it be scientific methodology or mathematical logic, must never be mistaken for a goal.

Samuel Meyer
1985

I

Bertrand Russell

My outlook on the world is, like other people's, the product partly of circumstance and partly of temperament. My father and mother were free-thinkers, but one of them died when I was two years old and the other when I was three, and I did not know their opinions until I grew up.

In 1876 after my father's death I was brought to the house of my grandparents. My grandmother was a Scotch Presbyterian. She was a more powerful influence upon my general outlook than anyone else. She was a Puritan, with the moral rigidity of the Covenanters, despising comfort, indifferent to food, hating wine, and regarding tobacco as sinful. On my twelfth birthday she gave me a Bible (which I still possess), and wrote her favorite texts on the fly-leaf. One of them was "Thou shalt not follow a multitude to do evil"; another, "Be strong, and of good courage; be not afraid, neither be thou dismayed, for the Lord thy God is with thee withersoever thou goest." These texts have profoundly influenced my life, and still seemed to retain some meaning after I had ceased to believe in God.

The first dogma which I came to disbelieve was that of free will. It seemed to me that all motions of matter were determined by the laws of dynamics and could not therefore be influenced by the human will, even in the instance of matter forming part of a human body. The next dogma which I began to doubt was that of immortality, but I cannot clearly remember what were at that time my reasons for disbelieving in it.

Indeed, it was at that very early age that one of the decisive experiences of my life occurred. My brother, who was seven years older than I was, undertook to teach me Euclid, and I was overjoyed—and I hoped at last to acquire some solid knowledge. I shall never forget my disappointment when I found that Euclid started with axioms. When my brother read the first axiom to me, I said that I saw no reason to admit it; to which he replied that such being the situation we could not go on. My belief that somewhere in the world solid knowledge was obtainable had received a rude shock.

My early attitude to mathematics was expressed in an article called "The Study of Mathematics." Some quotations from this essay illustrate what I then felt: "Mathematics, rightly viewed, possesses not only truth, but supreme beauty—a beauty cold and austere, like that of sculpture, without appeal to any part of our weaker nature, without the gorgeous trappings of painting or music, yet sublimely pure, and capable of a stern perfection such as only the greatest art can show."

All this has come to seem to me largely nonsense, partly for technical reasons and partly from a change in my general outlook upon the world. Mathematics has ceased to seem to me non-human in its subject-matter. I have come to believe, though very reluctantly, that it consists of tautologies. I fear that, to a mind of sufficient intellecutal power, the whole of mathematics would appear trivial, as trivial as the statement that a four-footed animal is an animal. I cannot any longer find any mystical satisfaction in the contemplation of mathematical truth.

My intellectual journeys have been, in some respects, disappointing. When I was young I hoped to find religious satisfaction in philosophy; even after I had abandoned Hegel, the eternal Platonic world gave me something non-human to admire. I have always ardently desired to find some justification for the emotions inspired by certain things that seemed to stand outside human life and to deserve feelings of awe—especially truth which like that of mathematics, does not merely describe the world that happens to exist. Those who attempt to make a religion of humanism, which recognizes nothing greater than man, do not satisfy my emotions. And yet I am unable to believe that, in the world as known, there is anything that I can value outside human beings. And so my intellect goes with the humanists, though my emotions violently rebel. In this respect, the "consolations of philosophy" are not for me.

The desire to discover some really certain knowledge inspired all my work up to the age of thirty-eight. It seemed clear that mathematics had a better claim to be considered knowledge than anything else. Then came the war, and I knew without the faintest shadow of doubt what I had to do. I have never been so wholehearted or so little troubled with hesitation in any work as in the pacifist work that I did during the war. For the first time I found something to do which involved my whole nature. A strong parental instinct, at that time not satisfied in a personal way, caused me to feel a great indignation at the spectacle of the young men of Europe being deceived and butchered in order to gratify the evil passions of their elders.

Intellectual integrity made it quite impossible for me to accept the war myths of any of the belligerent nations. If the intellectual has any function in society, it is to preserve a cool and unbiased judgment in the face of all solicitations to passion. I observed that at first most of those who stayed at home enjoyed the war, which showed me how much hatred and how little human affection exist in human nature educated on our present lines. I feared that European civilization would perish, as indeed it easily might have done if the war had lasted a year longer.

All my thinking on political, sociological and ethical questions during the last fifteen years has sprung from the impulse which came to me during the first days of the war. The supposed economic causes of war are in the nature of a rationalization. People wish to fight, and they therefore persuade themselves that it is to their interest to do so. The important question, then, is the psychological one—"Why do people wish to fight?" And this leads on from war to a host of other questions concerning impulses to cruelty and oppression in general and in turn involve a study of the origins of malevolent passions, and thence of psychoanalysis and the theory of education.

Being a pacifist forced one into opposition to the whole purpose of the community and made it very difficult to avoid a completely antinomian attitude of hostility to all recognized moral rules. My attitude, however, is not really one of hostility to moral rules; it is essentially that expressed by St. Paul. I do not always find myself in agreement with that apostle, but on this point my feeling is exactly the same as his—namely, that no obedience to moral rules can take the place of love, and that where love is genuine, it will, if combined with intelligence, suffice to generate whatever moral rules are necessary.

Translated into psychological terms, there may be an emotion of attraction or an emotion of fear. Both, of course, are necessary to survival, but emotions of fear are very much less necessary for survival in civilized life than they were at earlier stages of human development or among our pre-human ancestors.

At the present time the fiercest and most dangerous animal with which human beings have to contend is man—therefore, fear finds little scope except in relation to other human beings. It is a recognized maxim that the best defense is attack; consequently people are continually attacking each other because they expect to be attacked.

It is the conquest of nature which has made possible a more friendly and cooperative attitude between human beings, and if rational men cooperated and used their scientific knowledge to the full, they could now secure the economic welfare of all. With the problem of poverty and destitution eliminated, men could devote themselves to the constructive arts of civilization—to the progress of science, the diminution of disease, the postponement of death, the liberation of the impulses that make for joy.

Why do such ideas appear Utopian? The reasons lie solely in human psychology. The basis of international anarchy is man's proneness to fear and hatred. This is also the basis of economic disputes; for love of power, which is at their root, is generally an embodiment of fear. Men desire to be in control because they are afraid that the control of others will be used unjustly to their detriment. The same thing applies in the sphere of sexual morals: the power of husbands over wives and of wives over husbands, which is conferred by the law, is derived from fear of the loss of possession. This motive is the negative emotion of jealousy, not the positive emotion of love. In education the same kind of thing occurs. The positive emotion which should supply the motive in education is curiosity, but the curiosity of the young is severely repressed in many directions—sexual, theological, and political. Instead of being encouraged in the practice of free inquiry, children are instructed in some brand of orthodoxy, with the result that unfamiliar ideas inspire them with terror rather than with interest.

The road to Utopia is clear; it lies partly through politics and partly through changes in the individual. As for politics, far the most important thing is the establishment of an international government—a measure which I expect to be brought about through the world government of the United States. As for the individual, the problem is to make him less prone to hatred and fear. Much of the hatred in the world springs from bad digestion and inadequate functioning of the glands. In a world where the health of the young is adequately cared for and their vital impulses are given the utmost scope, compatible with their own health and that of their companions, men and women will grow up more courageous and less malevolent than they are at present.

II

John Dewey

In the Seventies, when I was an undergraduate, "electives" were still unknown in the smaller New England colleges. But in the one I attended, the University of Vermont, the tradition of a "senior-year course" still subsisted. This course was regarded as a kind of intellectual coping to the structure erected in the earlier years, or at least, as an insertion of the keystone of the arch. I have always been grateful for that year of my schooling. There was however, one course in the previous year that had excited a taste that in retrospect may be called philosophical. That was a rather short course, without laboratory work, in physiology, a book of Huxley's being the text. It is difficult to speak with exactitude about what happened to me intellectually so many years ago, but I have an impression that there was derived from that study a sense of interdependence and interrelated unity that gave form to intellectual stirrings that had been previously inchoate, and created a kind of type or model of a view of things to which material in any field ought to conform. Subconsciously, at least, I was led to desire a world and a life that would have the same properties as had the human organism in the picture of it derived from study of Huxley's treatment. I date from this time the awakening of a distinctive philosophic interest.

Teachers of philosophy were at that time, almost to a man, clergymen; the supposed requirements of religion, or theology, dominated the teaching of philosophy in most colleges. There was a firm alliance established between religion and the cause of "intuition." It is probably impossible to recover at this date the almost sacrosanct air that enveloped the idea of intuitions; but somehow the cause of all holy and valuable things was supposed to stand or fall with the validity of intuitionalism; the only vital issue was that between intuitionalism and a sensational empiricism that explained away the reality of all higher objects. The story of this almost forgotten debate, once so urgent, is probably a factor in developing in me a certain skepticism about the depth and range of purely contemporary issues; it is likely that many of those which seem highly important today will also in a generation have receded to the status of the local and provincial.

I do not mention this theological and intuitional phase because it had any lasting influence upon my own development, except negatively. I learned the terminology of an intuitional philosophy, but it did not go deep, and in no way did it satisfy what I was dimly reaching for.

I decided to make philosophy my life study, and accordingly went to Johns Hopkins in 1884 to enter upon that new thing, "graduate work." It was something of a risk; the work offered there was almost the only indication that there were likely to be any self-supporting jobs in the field of philosophy for others than clergymen. During the years after graduation I had kept up philosophical readings and I had even written a few articles which I sent to Dr. W.T. Harris, the well-known Hegelian and the editor of the Journal of Speculative Philosophy, the only philosophic journal in the country at that time.

The articles sent were, as I recall them, highly schematic and formal. My deeper interests had not as yet been met. I imagine that my development has been controlled largely by a struggle between a native inclination toward the schematic and formally logical, and those incidents of personal experience that compelled me to take account of actual material. Probably there is in the consciously articulated ideas of every thinker an overweighting of just those things that are contrary to his intrinsic bent, and which, therefore, he has to struggle to bring to expression, while the native bent, on the other hand, can take care of itself. Anyway, a case might be made out for the proposition that the emphasis upon the concrete, empirical, and "practical" in my later writings is partly due to considerations of this nature. It was a reaction against what was more natural, and it served as a protest and protection against something in myself which, in the pressure of the weight of actual experiences, I knew to be a weakness.

It is, I suppose, becoming a commonplace that when anyone is unduly concerned with controversy, the remarks that seem to be directed against others are really concerned with a struggle that is going on inside himself. The marks, the stigmata, of the struggle to weld together the characteristics of a formal, theoretic interest and the material of a maturing experience of contacts with realities also showed themselves, naturally, in style of writing and manner of presentation. During the time when the schematic interest predominated, writing was comparatively easy; there were even compliments upon the clearness of my style. Since then thinking and writing have been hard work. It is easy to give way to the dialectic development of a theme; the pressure of concrete experiences was, however, sufficiently heavy, so that a sense of intellectual honesty prevented a surrender to that course. But, on the other hand, the formal interest persisted, so that there was an inner demand for an intellectual technique that would be consistent and yet capable of flexible adaptation to the concrete diversity of experienced things. It is hardly necessary to say that I have not been among those to whom the union of abilities to satisfy these two opposed requirements, the formal and the material, came easily. For that very reason I have been acutely aware, too much so, doubtless, of a tendency of other thinkers and writers to achieve a specious lucidity and simplicity by the mere process of ignoring considerations which a greater respect for concrete materials of experience would have forced upon them.

There was a half-year of lecturing and seminar work given by Professor George Sylvester Morris; belief in the "demonstrated" (a favorite word of his) truth of the substance of German idealism, and belief in its competency to give direction to a life of aspiring thought, emotion, and action. I have never known a more single-hearted and whole-souled man—a man of a single piece all the way through; while I long since have deviated from his philosophic faith, I should be happy to believe that the influence of the spirit of his teaching has been an enduring influence.

While it was impossible that a young and impressionable student, unacquainted with any system of thought that satisfied his head and heart, should not have been deeply affected, to the point of at least a temporary conversion, by the enthusiastic and scholarly devotion of Mr. Morris, this effect was far from being the only source of my own "Hegelianism." The 'Eighties and 'Nineties were a time of new ferment in English thought; the reaction against atomic individualism and sensationalistic empiricism was in full swing. It was the time of Thomas Hill Green, of the two Cairds, of Wallace, of the appearance of the "Essays in Philosophical Criticism," co-operatively produced by a younger group under the leadership of the late Lord Haldane.

There were, however, also "subjective" reasons for the appeal that Hegel's thought made to me; it supplied a demand for unification that was doubtless an intense emotional craving, and yet was a hunger that only an intellectualized subject matter could satisfy. It is more than difficult, it is impossible, to recover that early mood. But the sense of divisions and separations that were, I suppose, borne in upon me as a consequence of a heritage of New England culture, divisions by way of isolation of self from the world, of soul from body, of nature from God, brought a painful oppression—or, rather, they were an inward laceration. My earlier philosophic study had been an intellectual gymnastic. Hegel's synthesis of subject and object, matter and spirit, the divine and the human, was, however, no mere intellectual formula; it operated as an immense release, a liberation. Hegel's treatment of human culture, of institutions, and the arts, involved the same dissolution of hard-and-fast dividing walls, and had a special attraction for me.

While the conflict of traditional religious beliefs with opinions that I could myself honestly entertain was the source of a trying personal crisis, it did not at any time constitute a leading philosophical problem. It was due to a feeling that any genuinely sound religious experience could and should adapt itself to whatever beliefs one found oneself intellectually entitled to hold—a half-unconscious sense at first, but one which ensuing years have deepened into a fundamental conviction. I have enough faith in the depth of the religious tendencies of men to believe that they will adapt themselves to any required intellectual change, and that it is futile (and likely to be dishonest) to forecast prematurely just what forms the religious interest will take as a final consequence of the great intellectual transformation that is going on.

In undergraduate days I had run across in the college library Harriet Martineau's exposition of Comte. His idea of the disorganized character of Western modern culture due to a disintegrative "individualism," and his idea of synthesis of science that should be a regulative method of an organized social life impressed me deeply.

I drifted away from Hegelianism in the next fifteen years. Nevertheless I should never think of ignoring, much less denying, what an astute critic occasionally refers to as a novel discovery—that acquaintance with Hegel has left a permanent deposit in my thinking. The form, the schematism, of his now seems to me artificial to the last degree. But in the content of his ideas, there is often an extraordinary depth. Were it possible for me to be a devotee of any system, I still should believe that there is greater richness and greater variety of insight in Hegel than in any other single systematic philosopher— though when I say this I exclude Plato, who still provides my favorite philosophic reading.

The rest of the story of my intellectual development I am unable to record without more faking than I care to indulge in. I envy, up to a certain point, those who can write their intellectual biography in a unified pattern, woven out of a few distinctly discernible strands of interest and influence. By contrast, I seem to be unstable, chameleon-like, yielding one after another to many diverse and even incompatible influences; struggling to assimilate something from each and yet striving to carry it forward in a way that is logically consistent with what has been learned from its predecessors.

The influence on my thinking by the publication of *Psychology* by William James was fundamental and vital. There are, I think, two unreconciled strains in the *Psychology*. One is the subjective tenor of prior psychological tradition; the point of view remained that of a realm of consciousness set off by itself. The other strain is objective, having its roots in a return to the earlier biological conception of the psyche. I doubt if we have as yet begun to realize all that is due to William James for the introduction and use of this idea. Anyway it worked its way more and more into all my ideas and acted as a ferment to transform old beliefs.

The point about the objective biological factor in James's conception of thought is fundamental when the role of psychology in philosophy comes under consideration. Historically the revolution introduced by James had, and still has, a peculiar significance. On the negative side it is important, for it is indispensable as a purge of the heavy charge of bad psychology that is so embedded in the philosophical tradition. As an example I would say that the problem of "sense data" which occupies such a great bulk in recent British thinking, has to my mind no significance other than as survival of an old and outworn psychological doctrine. On the positive side the newer objective psychology supplies the easiest way, pedagogically if not in the abstract, by which to reach a fruitful conception of thought and its work, and thus to better our logical theories—provided thought and logic have anything to do with one another. The more abstract sciences, mathematics and physics, for example, have left their impress deep upon traditional philosophy. The former in connection with an exaggerated anxiety about formal certainty has operated to divorce philosophic thinking from connection with questions that have a source in existence. The remoteness of psychology from such abstractions, its nearness to what is distinctively human, gives it an emphatic claim for a sympathetic hearing at the present time.

Intellectual prophecy is dangerous; but if I read the cultural signs of the times aright, the next synthetic movement in philosophy will emerge when the significance of the social sciences and arts has become an object of reflective attention in the same way that the mathematical and physical sciences have been made objects of thought in the past. Seen in the long perspective of the future, the whole of Western European history is a provincial episode. Meanwhile a chief task of those who call themselves philosophers is to help get rid of the useless lumber that blocks our highways of thought, and strive to make straight and open the paths that lead to the future. Forty yearts spent wandering in a wilderness is not a sad fate—unless one attempts to make himself believe that the wilderness is after all itself the promised land.

III

Russell on Dewey's "Logic: The Theory of Inquiry"

John Dewey is generally admitted to be the leading living philosopher of America. In this estimate I entirely concur. He has had a profound influence, not only among philosophers, but on students of education, aesthetics, and political theory. He is a man of the highest character, liberal in outlook, generous and kind in personal relations, indefatigable in work. With many of his opinions I am almost in complete agreement. Owing to my respect and admiration for him, as well as to personal experience of his kindness, I should wish to agree completely, but to my regret, I am compelled to dissent from his most distinctive philosophical doctrine, namely the substitution of "inquiry" for "truth" as the fundamental concept of logic and theory of knowledge.

Dr. Dewey has an outlook which, where it is distinctive, is in harmony with the age of industrialism and collective enterprise. It is natural that his strongest appeal should be to Americans, and also that he should be almost equally appreciated by the progressive elements in countries like China and Mexico, which are endeavoring to pass with great rapidity from medievalism to all that is most modern. His fame, though not his doctrine, is analogous to that enjoyed by Jeremy Bentham in his own day—except that Bentham was more respected abroad than by his compatriots.

In what follows, I shall not be concerned with these general matters, but only with one book: *Logic: The Theory of Inquiry.* This book is very rich and varied in its contents; it contains highly interesting criticisms of past philosophers, very able analyses of prejudices inspiring traditional formal logic, and an intimate awareness of the realities of scientific investigation. All this makes the book far more concrete than most books called "Logic." Since, however, a review should be shorter than the work reviewed, I shall ignore everything that occurs by way of illustration or history, and consider only those positive doctrines which seem to me most characteristic.

One of the chief sources of difference between philosophers is a temperamental bias towards synthesis or analysis. Traditionally, British philosophy was analytic, Continental philosophy synthetic. On this point, I find myself in the British tradition, while Dr. Dewey belongs with the Germans, and more particularly with Hegel. Instrumentalism, his most characteristic and important doctrine, is, I think, compatible with an analytic bias, but in him, it takes a form associated with what General Smuts calls "holism." Holism is the theory that the determining factors in nature are wholes (as organisms) which are irreducible to the sum of its parts—that is, a whole cannot be analyzed into the sum of its parts or reduced to discrete elements, as for example Gestalt psychology. I propose to consider first the "holistic" aspect of Dr. Dewey's logic, and the instrumental doctrine as he sets it forth.

Dr. Dewey himself has told of his debt to Hegel. He adds: "I should never think of ignoring, much less denying, what an astute critic occasionally refers to as a novel discovery—that acquaintance with Hegel has left a permanent deposit in my thinking."

Data, in the sense in which many empiricists believe in them, are rejected by Dr. Dewey as the starting point of knowledge. There is a process of "inquiry" in the course of which both subject and object change. The process is, in some degree, continuous throughout life. Nevertheless, in regard to any one problem, there is a beginning, and this beginning is called a "situation." A situation, we are told, is a "qualified existential whole which is unique."

There are a few further statements about what the world is apart from the effects which inquiry has upon it. For instance: "There is, of course, a natural world that exists independently of the organism, but this world is *environment* only as it enters directly and indirectly into life-functions." We are told very little about the nature of things before they are inquired into; we know, however, that, like dishonest politicians, things behave differently when observed from the way in which they behave when no one is paying attention to them.

The question arises: How large is a "situation"? In connection with historical knowledge, Dr. Dewey speaks of the "temporal continuity of past-present-future." It is obvious that, in an inquiry into the tides, the sun and the moon must be included in the "situation." Although this question is nowhere explicitly discussed, I do not see how, on Dr. Dewey's principles, a "situation" can embrace less than the whole universe; this is an inevitable consequence of the insistence upon continuity.

The relation of perception to empirical knowledge is not made very clear in this book. We are told that sense-data are not objects of knowledge, and have no objective existential reference. When it is said that sense-data have no objective existential reference, what is meant, no doubt, is that sensation is not a relational occurrence in which a subject cognizes something. To this I should entirely assent. Again we are told that there are three common errors to be avoided: (1) that the common-sense world is perceptual; (2) that perception is a mode of cognition; (3) that what is perceived is cognitive in status. Here again I agree. But since, clearly, perception is in some way related to empirical knowledge, a problem remains as to what this relation is.

I come now to what is most distinctive in Dr. Dewey's logic, namely the emphasis upon inquiry as opposed to truth or knowledge. Inquiry is not for him, as for most philosophers, a search for truth; it is an independent activity, defined as follows: "Inquiry is the controlled or directed transformation of an indeterminate situation into one that is so determinate in its constituent distinctions and relations as to convert the elements of the original situation into a unified whole." I cannot but think that this definition does not adequately express Dr. Dewey's meaning, since it would apply, for instance, to the operations of a drill-sergeant in transforming a collection of raw recruits into a regiment, or of a bricklayer transforming a heap of bricks into a house, and yet it would be impossible to say that the drill-sergeant is "inquiring" into the recruits, or the bricklayer, into the bricks. It is admitted that inquiry alters the object as well as the subject: "Inquiry is concerned with objective transformations of objective subject-matter." Propositions are merely tools in effecting these transformations; they are differentiated as means, not as "true" or "false."

I have pointed out elsewhere this doctrine's close similarity to that of another ex-Hegelian, Karl Marx, as stated in his *Theses on Feuerbach*, and afterwards embodied in the theory of dialectical materialism (which Engels never understood). "The question of whether objective truth belongs to human thinking is not a question of theory, but a practical question.

The truth, i.e. the reality and power, of thought must be demonstrated in practice. Philosophers have only *interpreted* the world in various ways, but the real task is to *alter* it."

"Truth" is not an important concept in Dr. Dewey's logic. I look up "truth" in the index and find only the following: "Defined, 345 (n). See Assertibility, Warranted." The note, in its entirety, is as follows:

"The best definition of *truth* from the logical standpoint which is known to me is that of Peirce: 'The opinion which is fated to be ultimately agreed to by all who investigate is what we mean by truth, and the object represented by this opinion is the real.' A more complete (and more suggestive) statement is the following: 'Truth is that concordance of an abstract statement with the ideal limit towards which endless investigation would tend to bring scientific belief, which concordance the abstract statement may possess by virtue of the confession of its inaccuracy and one-sidedness, and this confession is an essential ingredient of truth.' "

Although these definitions of "truth" are Peirce's, not Dr. Dewey's, the fact that Dr. Dewey accepts them makes it necessary to discuss them as if they were his own. If "truth" is to be so defined, it is obviously of no philosophical importance. The word "fated" seems merely rhetorical, and I shall assume that it is not intended seriously. But the word "ultimately" is much more difficult. The word is intended in a mathematical rather than a chronological sense. If it were intended chronologically it would make "truth" depend upon the opinions of the last man left alive as the earth becomes too cold to support life. As he will presumably be entirely occupied in keeping warm and getting nourishment, it is doubtful whether his opinions will be any wiser than ours. But obviously this is not what Peirce has in mind. He imagines a series of opinions, analogous to a series of numbers such as one-half, three-quarters, seven-eighths...tending to a limit, and each differing less from its predecessor than any earlier member of the series does. "The ideal limit towards which endless investigation would tend to bring scientific belief."

I find this definition exceedingly puzzling. To begin with a minor point: what is meant by "the confession of its inaccuracy"? Is "accuracy" a notion wholly divorced from "truth"? I think that Peirce, when he says "inaccurate," means "unprecise." The statement that Mr. A is about six feet tall may be perfectly accurate, but it is not precise. I think it is such statements that Peirce has in mind.

The main question is: Why does Peirce think that there is an "ideal limit towards which endless investigation would tend to bring scientific belief"? Does it contain any element of prophecy, or is it a merely hypothetical statement of what would happen if men of science grew continually cleverer? Whether the theory of relativity will be believed twenty years hence depends mainly upon whether Germany wins the next war. Whether it would be believed by people cleverer than we are we cannot tell without being cleverer than we are.

"Truth," therefore, as Peirce defines the term, is a vague concept involving much disputable sociology. Let us see what Dr. Dewey has to say about "assertibility warranted." He says: "If inquiry begins in doubt, it terminates in the institution of conditions which remove the need for doubt. The latter state of affairs may be designated by the words *belief* and *knowledge*. I prefer the words 'warranted assertibility.' " Again: "An inferential function is involved in all warranted assertion. The position here defended runs counter to the belief that there is such a thing as immediate knowledge, and that such knowledge is an indispensable precondition of all mediated knowledge."

Let us try to restate Dr. Dewey's theory in other language. I will begin with what would certainly be a misinterpretation, though one for which his words would seem to afford some justification. The position *seems* to be that there is a certain activity called "inquiry," as recognizable as the activities of eating or drinking; like all activity, it is stimulated by discomfort, and the particular discomfort concerned is called "doubt," just as hunger is the discomfort that stimulates eating, and thirst is the discomfort that stimulates drinking. And as hunger may lead you to kill an animal, skin it, and cook it, so that, though you have been concerned with the same animal throughout, it is very different when it becomes food for what it was to begin with, so inquiry manipulates and alters its subject-matter until it becomes logically assimilable and intellectually appetizing. Then doubt is allayed, at least for the time. But the subject-matter of inquiry, like the wild boar of Valhalla, is perpetually reborn, and the operation of logical cooking has to be more and more delicately performed as the intellectual palate grows more refined. There is therefore no end to the process of inquiry, and no dish that can be called "absolute truth."

I do not think that Dr. Dewey would accept what has just been said as an adequate account of his theory. He would, I am convinced, maintain that inquiry serves a purpose over and above the allaying of doubt. And he would object that the revival of an inquiry after doubt has been temporarily quieted is not merely a question of refinement of the intellectual palate, but has some more objective basis. He says: "If inquiry begins in doubt, it terminates in the institution of conditions which remove *need* for doubt." I do not know what he means by "need for doubt," but I think he means something more than "cause of doubt." If I doubt whether I am a fine fellow, I can cure the doubt by a suitable dose of alcohol, but this would not be viewed by him as "the institution of conditions which remove the *need* for doubt." Nor would he reckon suicide a suitable method, although it would be eminently effective in removing doubt. We must therefore ask ourselves what he can mean by "need for doubt."

For those who make "truth" fundamental, the difficulty in

question does not arise. There is need for doubt so long as there is an appreciable likelihood of a mistake. If you add up your accounts twice over, and get different results, there is "need for doubt"; but that is because you are persuaded that there is an objectively right result. If there is not, if all that is concerned is the psychological fact of inquiry as an activity stimulated by doubt, we cannot lay down rules as to what *ought* to remove the need for doubt: we can only observe what does in fact remove doubt. Inquiry will have to have some goal other than the removal of doubt.

The preface to Dr. Dewey's *Logic* contains the following passage: "The word 'Pragmatism' does not, I think, occur in the text. Perhaps the word lends itself to misconception. But in the proper interpretation of 'pragmatic,' namely the function of consequences as necessary tests of the validity of propositions, *provided* these consequences are operationally instituted and are such as to resolve the specific problem evoking the operations, the text that follows is thoroughly pragmatic."

Perhaps, in view of this passage, we may say that there is "need for doubt" so long as the opinion at which we have arrived does not enable us to secure desired results. When our car breaks down, we try various hypotheses as to what is wrong, and there is "need for doubt" until it goes again. This suggests a way out of our difficulty, which I will try to state in quite general terms.

Beliefs, we are now supposing, may be tested by their consequences, and may be considered to possess "warranted assertibility" when their consequences are of certain kinds. The consequences to be considered relevant may be logical consequences only, or may be widened to embrace all kinds of effects. In the case of the car that won't go, you think it may be this, or it may be that, or it may be the other; if it is *this* and I do so-and-so, the car will go; I do so-and-so and the car does not go; therefore it was not *this*. But when I apply the same experimental procedure to the hypothesis that it was *that*, the car does go; therefore the belief that it was *that* has "warranted assertibility." So far we have only the ordinary procedure of induction: "If p, then q; now q is true; therefore p is true." E.g., "If pigs have wings, then some winged animals are good to eat; now some winged animals are good to eat; therefore pigs have wings." This form of inference is called "scientific method."

As it stands, it is as follows: A hypothesis is called "true" when it leads the person entertaining it to acts which have effects that he desires. This obviously is too wide. Acts may have consequences of which some may be pleasant and others unpleasant. In the case of the car, it may, when it finally moves, move so suddenly that it causes you serious bodily injury; this does not show that you were mistaken as to what was the matter with it. Or take another illustration: In a school, a prize is offered for the child that shows most general intelligence; on class work, four are selected, and the final test is by a *viva voce*; the *viva* consists of one question, "Who is the greatest man now living?" One child says Roosevelt, one says Stalin, one says Hitler, and one says Mussolini. One of them gets the prize, and has therefore by definition, answered truly. If you know which gets the prize, you know in what country the test was made. It follows that truth is geographical. But this consequence, for some reason, pragmatists would be unwilling to admit.

There are still difficulties. Dr. Dewey and I were once in the town of Changsha during an eclipse of the moon; following immemorial custom, blind men were beating gongs to frighten the heavenly dog, whose attempt to swallow the moon is the cause of eclipses. Throughout thousands of years, this practice of beating gongs has never failed to be successful: every eclipse has come to an end after a sufficient prolongation of the din. This illustration shows that our generalization must not use merely the method of agreement, but also the method of difference.

Some beliefs which we should all hold to be false have

greatly helped success; for example the Mohammedan belief that the faithful who die in battle go straight to Paradise. When we reject this belief, do we mean merely that it proved an obstacle to science, and therefore to war-technique? Surely not. The question whether you will go to Paradise when you die is as definite as the question whether you will go to New York tomorrow. You would not decide this latter question by investigating whether those who believe they will go to New York tomorrow are on the whole more successful than those who do not. The test of success is only brought in where the usual tests fail. But *if* the Mohammedan belief was true, those who entertained it have long since had empirical evidence of its truth. *Such* evidence is convincing, but the argument from success is not.

There are certain general problems connected with such a theory as Dr. Dewey's, which perhaps deserve consideration although he does not discuss them. Inquiry, in his system, operates upon a raw material, which it gradually transforms; it is only the final product that can be known. The raw material remains an unknowable. That being the case, it is not quite clear why it is supposed to exist.

Perhaps the objections which I feel to the instrumentalist logic are merely emotional, and have no logical justification, although I am totally unable to believe that this is the case. Knowledge, if Dr. Dewey is right, cannot be any part of the ends of life; it is merely a means to other satisfactions. This view, to those who have been much engaged in the pursuit of knowlege, is distasteful. Dr. Dewey himself confesses to having felt this, and resisted it as a temptation. The emphasis upon the practical in his later writings, he says, "was a reaction against what was more natural, and it served as a protest and a protection against something in myself which, in the pressure of the weight of actual experience, I knew to be a weakness." Even those who doubt whether such asceticism is necessary either practically or theoretically, cannot but feel the highest respect for the moral force required to practice it consistently throughout a long span of years.

For my part, I believe that too great emphasis upon the practical robs practice itself of its *raison d'etre*. We act, insofar as we are not blindly driven by instinct, in order to achieve ends which are not merely further actions, but have in them some element, however precarious and however transient, of rest and peace—not the rest and peace of mere quiescence, but the kind that, in the most intense form, becomes ecstacy. When what passes for knowledge is considered to be no more than a momentary halting-place in a process of inquiry which has no goals outside itself, inquiry can no longer provide intellectual joys, but becomes merely a means to better dinners and more rapid locomotion. Activity can supply only one half of wisdom; the other half depends upon a receptive passivity. Ultimately, the controversy between those who base logic upon "truth" and those who base it upon "inquiry" arises from a difference of values, and cannot be argued without, at some point, begging the question. I cannot hope, therefore, that anything I have said, or written, has validity except for those whose bias resembles my own, while those whose bias resembles Dr. Dewey's will find in his book just such an exposition as the subject seems to them to require.

IV

Dewey's Reply to Russell

Among the contemporary factors which enable us to get away from issues that lack present support and relevance is the influence of biology and cultural anthropology in transforming traditional psychological views. The point to be borne in mind in this connection is the respective bearings of the old "subjectivistic" psychology and the new behavioral one upon the philosophical conception of experience. It is to me a very curious fact that some of my critics take for granted a mentalistic view of experience; so that they cannot help attributing to me that view when I speak of experience. In addition they so largely ignore the difficulties inherent in their own subjectivism. The biological-anthropological method of approach to experience provides the way out of mentalistic into behavioral interpretation of experiencing. With equal necessity and per-

47

tinency, it points the way out of the belief that experience as such is inherently cognitional and that cognition is the sole path that leads it to the natural world.

The other fundamental consideration is drawn from a study of modern scientific method in its contrast with Greek and medieval theory and practice of knowing. It is, of course, the importance of the experimental method. If in this connection I have emphasized physical knowledge, it is not (as I have said many times) because the latter is the only kind of knowledge, but because its comparative maturity exemplifies so conspicuously the necessary place and function of experimentation; whereas, in contrast, beliefs in moral and social subjects are still reached and framed with minimum regard for experimental method.

I am aware that it is now not unusual to say that the value of experimental method is such a familiar commonplace that it is not necessary to dwell upon its implications; that putting it in antithesis to the theory of immediate knowing is but a case of slaying the dead. I wish this were so. If it were, I should feel that I had accomplished a large part of the purpose I set out to accomplish. But I find the belief in immediate knowledge still flourishing, and I also find that a writer like Mr. Bertrand Russell can link my theory of knowledge and the place of experimentation (doing and making) in knowledge primarily with an age of industrialism and collective enterprise, so especially marked in this country as to make my philosophy peculiarly American. This view is a repetition of a position he took long ago when, in 1922, he said that he found the "love of truth obscured in America by commercialism of which pragmatism is the philosophical expression." I remarked that the statement seemed to me to be "of that order of interpretation which would say that English neo-realism is a reflection of the snobbish aristocracy of the English and the tendency of French thought to dualism an expression of an alleged Gallic disposition to keep a mistress in addition to a wife; and the idealism of

Germany a manifestation of an ability to elevate beer and sausage into a higher synthesis with the spiritual values of Beethoven and Wagner." And I still believe that Mr. Russell's confirmed habit of connecting the pragmatic theory of knowing with the obnoxious aspects of American industrialism, instead of with the experimental method of attaining knowledge, is much as if I were to link his philosophy to the interests of English landed aristocracy instead of with dominant interest in mathematics.

Other criticisms of my theory of experience are connected with the fact that I have called experiences *situations*, my use of the word antedating, I suppose, the introduction of the *field* idea in physical theory, but nevertheless employed, as far as I can see, to meet pretty much the same need—a need imposed by subject matter not by theory. The need in both cases— though with different subject-matters—is to find a viable alternative to an atomism and to an absolutistic block monism. In philosophy there is also the need to find an alternative for that combination of atomistic particularism with respect to empirical materialism and Platonic *a priori* realism with respect to universals which is professed, for example, in the philosophy of Mr. Russell. According to the naturalistic view, every experience in its direct occurrence is an interaction of environing conditions and an organism. In other words, the theory of experiential situations which follows directly form the biological-anthropological approach is by its very nature a *via media* between extreme atomistic pluralism and block universe monisms. Which is but to say that it is genuinely empirical in a naturalistic sense.

Mr. Russell, however, finds what I write about situations as the units of experience springs from and leads directly to the Hegelian variety of absolutism. One indirect reason he presents for this belief, when it is put in the form of an argument, runs somewhat as follows: Mr. Dewey admits not only that he was once an Hegelian but that Hegel left a permanent deposit in his thought; Hegel was a thoroughgoing holist; therefore Dewey uses "situation" in a holistic sense. I leave it to Mr. Russell as a formal logician to decide what he would say to anyone who presented this argument in any other context. The following argument answers perhaps more to Mr. Russell's idea of inductive reasoning. British philosophy is analytic; Dewey not only leans to the Continental synthetic tendency but has vigorously criticized British analytic thought; therefore his identification of an experience with a situation commits him to "holism."

Coming to a more relevant matter, the interpretation put by Mr. Russell upon quotations of passages in which I have used the word *situation* contradicts what, according to my basic leading principle, is designated by it. This position, however, is not just a necessary implication of that principle. The pluralistic and individualized character of situations is stated over and over again, and is stated moreover in direct connection with the principle of experimental continuum. Take for instance the following passage:

"Situations are precarious and perilous because the persistance of life-activity depends upon the influence which present acts have upon future acts. The *continuity* of a life process is secured only as acts performed render the environment favorable to subsequent organic acts.... All perceived objects are individualized. They are, as such, wholes complete in themselves. Every thing directly experienced is qualitatively unique." (*Quest for Certainty*, 234.)

I lay no claim to inventing an environment that is marked by both discreteness and continuity. Nor can I even make the more modest claim that I discovered it. What I have done is to interpret this duality of traits in terms of the identity of experience with life-functions. For in the process of living both absorption in a present situation and a response that takes account of its effect upon the conditions of later experiences are equally necessary for maintenance of life. From one angle, almost everything I have written is a commentary on the fact that situations are *immediate* in their direct occurrence, and mediating and mediated in the temporal continuum constituting life-experience.

The horse led to water is not forced to drink. This predicament has to be faced by the experimentalist in physical inquiry. He can describe the experimental set-up, the material involved, the apparatus employed, the series of acts performed, the observations which result and state the conclusions reached. But even so it is up to other inquirers to take this report as an invitation to *have* a certain experienced situation and as a direction as to how to obtain it. Anyone who refuses to go outside the universe of discourse—as Mr. Russell apparently does—has of course shut himself off from understanding what a "situation," as directly experienced subject-matter, is.

An almost humorous instance of such refusal and its consequences is found when Mr. Russell writes: "We are told very little about the nature of things before they are inquired into." If I have said or tried to say the tiniest bit about the "nature of things" prior to inquiry into them, I have not only done something completely contradictory to my own position but something that seems to me inherently absurd. Whatever Mr. Russell may have meant by the sentence quoted, my position is that *telling* is (i) a matter of discourse, and that (ii) all discourse is derived from and inherently referable to experiences of things in non-discursive experiential having; so that, for example, although it is possible to tell a man blind from birth *about* color, we cannot by discourse confer upon him that which is had in the direct experience of color—my whole position on this matter being a generalization of this commonplace fact.

When Mr. Russell adds to the sentence just quoted from him, the phrase "we know, however, that, like dishonest politicians, things behave differently when observed from the way they behave when no one is paying attention to them," I do not suppose he is intending to say that, according to the Heisenberg principle, minute particles moving at high velocities behave like dishonest politicians. I take it he is referring to something he regards as a legitimate inference from my position. In the latter case, it is probably well for me to state once more what my view is. It is that scientific knowledge has an effect upon things *previously directly-experienced-but-not-known*. Now this I should have supposed to be a commonplace, although a commonplace which philosophers have mostly not deigned to notice.

I have not been guilty of the Irish bull with which I am occasionally charged. I have not held, as is intimated in Mr. Russell's allusion to knowledge of sun and planets, that knowing modifies the *object of knowledge*. That a planet *as known* is a very different thing from the speck of light that is found in direct experience, I should suppose to be obvious; although, once more, one of those commonplaces of which philosophers engaged in pursuit of an artificial problem have failed to take proper note. The fact that critics so readily forget that the planet, rock (or whatever it is they imagine I hold to be modified by knowing) is *already* an object of knowledge indicates that they hold that the entire subject-matter of philosophical theory is exhaustively contained within the field of discourse. An empiricist will hold that subject-matter to be *philosophically* understood has to be placed in its reference to subject-matter of directly experienced situations. Stated in another way, the material of sensations, impressions, ideas as copies, etc. with which traditional empiricism has operated is material already taken out of the context of direct experience and placed in the context of material within discourse for the purpose of meeting the requirements of discourse.

In this connection Mr. Russell's belief that I hold that the "raw material remains *unknowable*" is peculiarly indicative. For it affords final proof that Mr. Russell has not been able to follow the distinction I make between the immediately had material of non-cognitively experienced situations and the material of cognition—a distinction without which my view cannot be understood. A typical illustration of what I mean by such non-cognitive experiences would be things experienced by way of love, desire, hope, fear and other traits characteristic of human individuality. Instead, however, holding that this material is *unknowable*, my view is that when the situations in which such material exists become *problematic*, it provides precisely that which is *to be* known by being inquired into. But apparently Mr. Russell is so wedded to the idea that there is no experienced material outside the field of discourse that any intimation that there is such material relegates it, *ipso facto*, to the status of the "*unknowable.*"

Although the point now to be explicitly mentioned concerns my theory of knowledge rather than my theory of experience, it is so directly connected with the "holistic" meaning Mr. Russell reads into the word "situation" as used by me, that it is taken up here. Mr. Russell asserts that my use of the word "situation" commits me to the view that the entire universe is the only "real" object of knowledge, so that logically I am committed to the view expressed by Bradley. It so happens that I have explicitly stated the fundamental difference between my view and that of the Bradleyan type. I quote the passage because it shows, unless I am mistaken, that the source of Russell's misconception of my view is his imperviousness to what I have said about the *problematic* quality of situations as giving both the occasion for and the control of inquiry.

"The theory (that is, of the type just mentioned) thus radically misconstrues the unification towards which inquiry in its reflective mediate stage actually moves. In actual inquiry, movement toward a unified ordered situation exists. But it is always a unification of the subject-matter which constitutes an *individual problematic situation*. It is not unification at large."

If, however, "the feature of unification is generalized beyond the limits in which it takes place, namely *resolution of specific problematic situations*, knowledge is then supposed to consist of attainment of a final all-comprehensive Unity, equivalent to the Universe as an unconditioned whole." (Logic 531.)

The passage (just quoted), however, is almost at the close of the book so that it may have escaped Mr. Russell's attention.

V

Russell's Rejoinder to Dewey

In recent philosophy there are varying types of theory as to "truth" or its replacement by some concept which is thought preferable. The theory which substitutes "warranted assertibility" for "truth" is advocated by Dr. Dewey and his school. This theory differs radically from the theory that I advocate and must therefore be discussed. I wish to confine myself to the general principle, and to consider it as uncontroversially as is compatible with giving my reasons for rejecting it.

It appears from Dr. Dewey's reply that I have unintentionally misunderstood and parodied his opinions. I am most anxious to avoid doing so if I possibly can, the more so as I am convinced that there is an important difference between his views and mine, which will not be elicited unless we can understand each other. It is because the difference goes deep that it is difficult to find words which both sides can accept as a fair statement of the issue. This, however, is what I must attempt.

So far as I can understand Dr. Dewey, his theory is, in outline, as follows. Among the various kinds of activities in which mankind can engage, there is one called "inquiry," of which the general purpose, like that of many other kinds of activity, is to increase the mutual adaptation of men and their environment. Inquiry uses "assertions" as its tools, and assertions are "warranted" in so far as they produce the desired results. But in inquiry, as in any other practical operation better tools may, from time to time, be invented, and the old ones are then discarded. Indeed, just as machines can enable us to make better machines, so the temporary results of an inquiry may be the very means which lead to better results. In this process there is no finality, and therefore no assertion is warranted for all time, but only at a given stage of inquiry. "Truth" as a static concept is therefore to be discarded.

The following passage in Dr. Dewey's reply to me may serve to elucidate his point of view:

"The exclusive devotion of Mr. Russell to discourse is manifested in his assumption that *propositions* are the subject-matter of inquiry, a view assumed so unconsciously that it is taken for granted that Peirce and I likewise assume it. But according to our view—and according to that of any thoroughgoing empiricist—*things and events* are the material and objects of inquiry, and propositions are *means* in inquiry, so that as conclusions of a given inquiry they become means of carrying on further inquiries. Like other means they are modified and improved in the course of use. Given the beliefs (i) that propositions are from the start the objects of inquiry and (ii) that all propositions have either truth or falsity as their inherent property, and (iii) then read these two assumptions into theories—like Peirce's and mine—which deny both of them, and the product is just the doctrinal confusion that Russell finds in what we have said."

First a few words of personal explanation. Any reader of the present work will, I hope be convinced that I do not make *propositions* the ultimate subject-matter of inquiry, since my problem has been, throughout, the relation between *events* and the propositions that they cause men to assert. I do not, it is true, regard *things* as the object of inquiry since I hold them to be metaphysical delusion; but as regards *events* I do not, on this point, disagree with Dr. Dewey. Again: as regards scientific hypotheses, such as quantum theory or the law of gravitation, I am willing (with some qualifications) to accept his view, but I regard all such hypotheses as a precarious superstructure built on a foundation of simpler and less dubious beliefs, and I do not find in Dr. Dewey's work what seems to me an adequate discussion of this foundation.

As to truth and falsehood, I should interpret the facts as regards inquiries and changing hypotheses somewhat differently. I should say that inquiry begins, as a rule, with an assertion that is vague and complex, but replaces it, when it can, by a number of separate assertions each of which is less vague and less complex than the original assertion. A complex assertion may be analyzable into several, some true, some false: A vague assertion may be true or false, but it is often neither. "An elephant is smaller than a mouse" is vague, and yet definitely false but "a rabbit is smaller than a rat" is not definitely either true or false, because some young rabbits are smaller than some old rats.

When Newton's theory of gravitation was replaced by Einstein's a certain vagueness in Newton's concept of acceleration was removed, but almost all the assertions implied by Newton's theory remained true. I should say that this is an illustration of what always happens when an old theory gives way to a better one: The old assertions failed to be definitely true or false, both because they were vague, and because they were many masquerading as one, some of the many being true and some false. But I do not see how to state the improvement except in terms of the two ideals of precision and truth.

One difficulty, to my mind, in Dr. Dewey's theory, is raised by the question: What is the goal of inquiry? The goal, for him, is not the attainment of truth, but presumably some kind of harmony between the inquirer and his environment. I have raised this question before, but have not seen any answers to it. Other activities, such as building houses, or printing newspapers or manufacturing bombs, have recognizable purposes. In regard to them, the difference between a good tool and a bad one is obvious: A good tool minimizes the labor involved in achieving the purpose. But "inquiry" is neutral as between different aims: Whatever we wish to do, some degree of inquiry is necessary as a preliminary. If I wish to telephone to a friend, I must inquire his number of the telephone book, taking care to use the most recent edition, since its truths are not eternal. If I wish to govern the country, I must inquire in previously unfamiliar circles as to how to become a political boss. If I wish to build ships, either I or someone in my employ must inquire into hydrostatics. If I wish to destroy democracy, I must inquire into crowd psychology. And so on. The question is: What happens as the result of my inquiry? Dr. Dewey rejects the traditional answer, that I come to *know* something, and that as a consequence of my knowledge, my actions are more successful. He eliminates the intermediate stage of "knowing" and says that the only essential result of successful inquiry is successful action.

Taking man as he appears to science, and not as he may appear to a Cartesian skeptic, there are here two questions to be discussed. First: What sort of psychological occurrence is to be described as a "believing"? Second: Is there any relation between a "believing" and its environment which allows us to call the believing "true"? To each of these questions I have tried to give an answer. If there are such occurrences as "believings" which seems undeniable, the question is: Can they be divided into two classes, the "true" and the "false"? Or, if not, can they be so analyzed that their constituents can be divided into these two classes? If either of these questions is answered in the affirmative, is the distinction between "true" and "false" to be found in the success or failure of the effects of believings, or is it to be found in some other relation which they may have to relevant occurrences?

I am prepared to admit that a belief as a whole may fail to be either "true" or "false" because it is compounded of several, some true, and some false. I am also prepared to admit that some beliefs fail, through vagueness, to be either true or false, though others, in spite of vagueness, are either true or false. Further than this I cannot go towards agreement with Dr. Dewey.

In Dr. Dewey's view, a belief is "warranted" if, as a tool, it is useful in some activity, i.e. if it is a cause of satisfaction of desire. This, at least, would have seemed to me to be his opinion. But he points out that consequences are only to be accepted as tests of validity "*provided* these consequences are operationally instituted and are such as to resolve the specific problem evoking the operations" (loc. cit., p. 571). The second half of this proviso is clear in its meaning. If I go to a place under the mistaken belief that my long-lost uncle lives there, but on the way I meet my long-lost aunt, and in consequence she leaves me her fortune, that does not prove that "my long-lost uncle lives there" had "warranted assertibility." But the first half of the proviso, which insists that the consequences must be "operationally instituted," is one of which the meaning remains to me somewhat obscure. The passage in Dr. Dewey's "Logic" (Preface, p. iv) where the phrase occurs does not elucidate it. But in his reply to me there is a passage which I will quote in full, as it is designed to remove my errors in interpretation:

"The proviso about the kind of consequences that operate as tests of validity was inserted as a caution against just the kind of interpretation which Mr. Russell gives to my use of consequences. For it explicitly states that it is necessary that they be *such as to resolve the specific problem* undergoing investigation. The interpretation Mr. Russell gives to consequences relates them to personal desire. The net outcome is attribution to me of a generalized wishful thinking as a definition of truth. Mr. Russell proceeds, first by converting a doubtful *situation* into a personal doubt, although the difference between the two things is repeatedly pointed out by me. I have even explicitly stated that a personal doubt is pathological unless it is a reflection of a *situation* which is problematic. Then by changing doubt into private discomfort, truth is identified with removal of this discomfort. The only desire that enters, according to my view, is desire to resolve as honestly and impartially as possible the problem involved in the situation. 'Satisfaction' is satisfaction of the conditions prescribed by the problem. Personal satisfaction may enter in as it arises when any job is well done according to the requirements of the job itself; but it does not enter in any way into the determination of validity, because on the contrary, it is determined by that validity."

I find this passage very puzzling. Dr. Dewey *seems* to speak as if a doubtful situation could exist without a personal doubter. I cannot think that he means this; he cannot intend to say, for example, that there were doubtful situations in astronomical and geological epochs before there was life. The only way in which I can interpret what he says is to suppose that, for him, a "doubtful situation" is one which arouses doubt, not only in some one individual, but in any normal man, or in any man anxious to achieve a certain result, or in any scientifically trained observer engaged in investigating the situation. *Some* purpose, i.e. *some* desire, is involved in the idea of a doubtful situation. If my car won't go, that creates a doubtful situation if I want it to go, but not if I want to leave it where it is. The only way to eliminate all reference to *actual* desire is to make the desire purely hypothetical: A situation is "doubtful" in relation to a given desire if it is not known what, in that situation, must be done to satisfy that desire. When I say, "It is not known," I must mean, in order to avoid the sort of subjectivity that Dr. Dewey depreciates, that it is not known to those who have the relevant training. Thus suppose I find myself in a situation S, and I desire a situation S', and I believe (rightly or wrongly) that there is something that I could do which would transform S into S', but the experts cannot tell me what to do, then S is, in relation to my desire, a "doubtful" situation.

Eliminating all reference to personal doubt and desire, we may now say: S is "doubtful" in relation to S' if mankind do not know of any human action A which will transform S into S', but also do not know that no such action is possible. The process of inquiry will consist in performing a series of actions A, A', A"...in the hope that one of them will transform S into S'. This, of course, implies that S and S' are both described in terms of universals, since, otherwise, neither can occur more than once. A, A', A"...must also be so described, since we wish to arrive at some such statement as: "Whenever you are in the situation S, and wish to be in the situation S', you can secure your desire by performing the action A", where A must be a *kind* of action, since otherwise it could only be performed once.

Thus when we take Dr. Dewey's elimination of subjective desire seriously, we find that his goal is to discover causal laws of the old sort, "C causes E," except that C must be a situation plus an act, and E another situation. These causal laws, if they are to serve their purpose, must be "true" in the very sense that Dr. Dewey wishes to abolish.

One important difference between us arises, I think, from the fact that Dr. Dewey is mainly concerned with theories and hypotheses, where I am mainly concerned with assertions about particular matters of fact. As explained prior to this, I hold that for any empirical theory of knowledge, the fundamental assertions must be concerned with particular matters of fact, i.e. with single events which only happen once. Unless there is *something* to be learnt from a single event, no hypothesis can ever be either confirmed or confuted; but what is to be learnt from a single event must itself be incapable of being confirmed or confuted by subsequent experience. This whole question of how we learn historical facts by experience seems to me to be ignored by Dr. Dewey and the school of which he is the leader. Take for instance the statement "Caesar was assassinated." This is true in virtue of a single event which happened long ago; nothing that has happened since or will happen in the future can in any way affect its truth or falsehood.

The distinction between truth and knowledge, which was emphasized in connection with the law of excluded middle, is relevant at this point. If I wish to "verify" the statement "Caesar was assassinated," I can only do so by means of *future* events—consulting books of history, manuscripts, etc. But these are only to the purpose as affording evidence of something other than themselves. When I make the statement, I do not mean, "Whoever looks up the encyclopaedia will find certain black marks on white paper." My seeing these black marks is a unique event on each occasion when I see them; on each occasion I can know that I have seen them; from this knowledge I can infer (more or less doubtfully) that Caesar was assassinated. But my perception of the black marks and my inference from this perception are not what makes the assertion about Caesar *true*. It would be true even if I made it without any grounds whatever. It is true because of what happened long ago, not because of anything that I am doing or shall do.

The broad issue may be stated as follows. Whether we accept or reject the words "true" and "false," we are all agreed that assertions can be divided into two kinds, sheep and goats. Dr. Dewey holds that a sheep may become a goat, and vice versa, but admits the dichotomy at any given moment: The sheep have "warranted assertibility" and the goats have not. Dr. Dewey holds that the division is to be defined by the *effects* of assertions, while I hold, at least as regards empirical assertions, that it is to be defined by their *causes*. An empirical assertion which can be *known* to be true has percepts, or a percept, among its proximate or remote causes. But this only applies to knowledge; so far as the *definition* of truth is concerned, causation is only relevant in conferring meaning upon words.

VI

Dewey's Rebuttal to Russell's
"An Inquiry into Meaning and Truth"

I propose to restate some features of the theories I have previously advanced on the basis of ascriptions and criticisms of my views found in Mr. Russell's book "An Inquiry into Truth and Meaning." I am in full agreement with his statement that "there is an important difference between his views and mine, which will not be elicited unless we can understand each other." Indeed, I think the statement might read, "We cannot understand each other unless important differences between us are brought out and borne in mind."

Mr. Russell refers to my theory as one which "substitutes 'warranted assertibility' for truth." Under certain conditions, I should have no cause to object to this reference. But the conditions are absent; and it is possible that this view of "substitution" plays an important role in generating what I take to be misconceptions of my theory. Hence, I begin by saying that my analysis of "warranted assertibility" is offered as a *definition* of the nature of knowledge according to which only *true* beliefs are knowledge. As I wrote in my *Logic: The Theory of Inquiry*, "What has been said helps explain why the term 'warranted assertibility' is preferred to the terms *belief* and *knowledge*. It is free from the ambiguity of the latter term."

For example, Mr. Russell says, "One important difference between us arises, I think, from the fact that Dr. Dewey is mainly concerned with theories and hypotheses, whereas I am mainly concerned with assertions about particular matters of fact." My position is that something of the order of a theory or hypothesis is demanded, if there is to be *warranted* assertibility in the case of a particular matter of fact. This position gives an importance to ideas (theories, hypotheses) they do not have upon Mr. Russell's view. But it is not about matters of particular fact since it states the *conditions* under which we reach warranted assertibility about particular matters of fact.

My view holds that the presence of an *idea* is required for any assertion entitled to rank as knowledge or as true; the insistence that the "presence" be by way of an existential operation demarcates it from most other such theories. I may indicate some of my reasons for taking this position by mentioning some difficulties in the contrasting view of Mr. Russell that there are propositions known in virtue of their own immediate direct presence, as in the case of "There is red," or as Mr. Russell prefers to say, "Redness-here."

(i) I do not understand how "here" has a self-contained and self-assured meaning save as discriminated from *there*, while *there* seems to me to be plural; a matter of manifold *theres*. These discriminations involve, I believe, determinations going beyond anything directly given or capable of being directly present. I would even say that a theory involving determination or definition of what is called "space" is involved in the allegedly simple "redness-here."

(ii) If I understand Mr. Russell aright, he holds that the ultimacy and purity of basic propositions is connected with (possibly is guaranteed by) the fact that subject-matters like "redness-here" are of the nature of perceptual experiences, in which perceptual material is reduced to a direct *sensible* presence, or *sensum*. For example he writes: "We can, however, in theory, distinguish two cases in relation to a judgment such as 'That is red'; one when it is caused by what it asserts, and the other, when words or images enter into its causation. In the former case, it must be true; in the latter case it may be false." Mr. Russell goes on to ask: "What can be meant when we say a 'percept' causes a word or sentence? On the face of it, we have to suppose a considerable process in the brain, connecting visual centers with motor centers; the causation, therefore, is by no means direct." Upon Mr. Russell's own view a quite elaborate physiological theory intervenes in any given case as condition of assurance that "redness-here" is a true assertion. I may add that a theory regarding causation also seems to be intimately involved. In view of such considerations as these, any view which holds that all complex propositions depend for their status *as knowledge* upon prior atomic propositions, of the nature described by Mr. Russell, seems to me the most adequate foundation yet provided for complete skepticism.

The position which I take, namely that all knowledge or warranted assertion depends upon inquiry and that inquiry is connected with what is questionable (and questioned) involves a skeptical element, or what Peirce called "fallibilism." But it also provides for *probability*, and for determination of degrees of probability in rejecting all intrinsically dogmatic statements, where "dogmatic" applies to *any* statement asserted to possess inherent self-evident truth. That the only alternative to ascribing to some propositions self-sufficient, self-possessed, and self-evident truth is a theory which finds the test and mark of truth in *consequences* of some sort is, I hope, an acceptable view.

In an earlier passage Mr. Russell ascribes certain views to "instrumentalists" and points out certain errors which undoubtedly (and rather obviously) exist in those views—as *he* conceives and states them. The passage reads:

"There are some schools of philosophy—notably the Hegelians and the instrumentalists—which deny the distinction between data and inference altogether. They maintain that in all our knowledge there is an inferential element, that truth is an organic whole and that the test of truth is coherence rather than conformity with 'fact.' I do not deny an element of truth in this view, but I think that, if taken as a whole truth, it renders the part played by perception inexplicable. It is surely obvious that every perceptive experience affords me either new knowledge or at least, as in the case of eclipses, greater certainty than I could have previously obtained by means of inference. To this the instrumentalist replies that any statement of the new knowledge obtained from perception is always an interpretation based upon accepted theories and may need subsequent correction if these theories turn out to be unsuitable."

I begin with the ascription to instrumentalists of the idea that "in all our knowledge, there is an inferential element." This statement is (from the standpoint of my view) ambiguous; in one of its meanings, it is incorrect. According to my view, while to infer something is necessary if a warranted assertion is to be arrived at, this inferred somewhat never appears *as such* in the latter, that is, in knowledge. The inferred material has to be checked and tested. The means of testing, required to give an inferential element any claim whatsoever to be *knowledge* instead of conjecture, are the data provided by observation— and only observation. The necessity of both the distinction and the cooperation of inferential and observational subject-matters is, on my theory, the product of an analysis of scientific inquiry; this necessity is the heart of my whole theory that knowledge is warranted assertion.

Instead of holding that "accepted theories" are always the basis for interpretation of what is newly obtained in perceptual experience, the instrumentalist points out that such a mode of interpretation is a common and serious source of wrong conclusions: of dogmatism and of consequent arrest of advance in knowledge. In my *Logic*, I have explicitly pointed out that one chief reason why the introduction of experimental methods meant such a great, such a revolutionary, change in natural science, is that they provide data which are new not only in detail but in *kind*. Hence their introduction compelled new kinds of inference to new kinds of subject-matters, and the formation of new types of theories.

I am obliged to form a certain hypothesis as to how and why, in view of the oft-repeated statements in my *Logic* of the *necessity* for distinguishing between inferential elements and observational data, it could occur to anyone that I denied the distinction. The best guess I can make is that my statements were not taken seriously because it was supposed that upon my theory these data themselves represent *cases of knowledge*, so that there must be on my theory an inferential element also in them. Whether or not this is the source of the alleged denial thought up by Mr. Russell, it may be used to indicate a highly significant difference between our two views. For Mr. Russell holds, if I understand him, that propositions about these data are in some cases instances of knowledge, and indeed that such cases provide, as basic propositions, the model upon which a theory of truth should be formed. In my view, they are not cases of knowledge although propositional formulation of them is a *necessary* (but not sufficient) condition of knowledge.

I can understand that my actual view may seem even more objectionable to a critic than the one that has been wrongly ascribed to me. The view imputed to me is that "inquiry uses 'assertions' as its tools, and assertions are 'warranted' insofar as they produce the desired results."

Propositions are means, instrumentalities, since they are the operational agencies by which *beliefs* that have adequate grounds for acceptance are reached as *ends* of inquiry. The difference between the instrumentality of a *proposition* as a means of attaining a grounded *belief* and the instrumentality of a *belief* as means of reaching certain "*desired results*" should be fairly obvious, independently of acceptance or rejection of my view.

Knowledge is in every case connected with inquiry. The conclusion or end of inquiry has to be demarcated from the intermediate means by which inquiry goes forward to a warranted or justified conclusion. The intermediate means are formulated in discourse as propositions and that means they have the properties appropriate to means (relevancy and efficacy).

It will be clear that truth and falsity are properties only of that subject-matter which is the *end*, the close of inquiry by means of which it is reached. The distinction between true and false conclusions is determined by the character of the operational procedures.

My view of the nature of propositions, as distinct from that held by Mr. Russell, may be further illustrated by commenting upon the passage in which referring to my view he writes: "I should say that inquiry begins, as a rule, with an assertion that is vague and complex, but replaces it, when it can, by a number of separate assertions each of which is less vague and less complex than the original assertion." I remark in passing that previous observations of this kind by Mr. Russell were what led me so to misapprehend his views as to impute to him the assumption "that *propositions* are the subject-matter of inquiry"; an impression, which, if it were not for his present explicit declaimer, would be strengthened by reading, "When we embark upon an inquiry we assume that *the propositions about which we are inquiring* are either true or false."

I would say that upon my view "propositions are *not* that about which we are inquiring," and that as far as we do find it necessary or advisable to inquire about them, it is not their truth and falsity about which we inquire, but the relevancy and efficacy of their subject-matter with respect to the problem in hand.

Accepting Mr. Russell's statement that his "problem has been, throughout, the relation between events and propositions," I would point out what seems to be a certain indeterminateness in his view of the relation between events and propositions, and the consequent need of introducing a distinction: viz., the distinction between the problem of the relation of events and propositions *in general*, and the problem of the relation of a particular proposition to the *particular* event to which it purports to refer. I can understand that Mr. Russell holds that certain propositions, of a specified kind, are such direct effects of certain events, and of nothing else, that they "must be true." But this view does not, as I see the matter, answer the question of how we know that *in a given case* this direct relationship actually exists. It does not seem to me that his theory gets beyond specifying the kind of case *in general* in which the relation between an event, as causal antecedent, and a proposition, as effect, is such as to confer upon instances of the latter the property of being true.

In the case, previously cited, of *redness-here*, Mr. Russell asserts that it is true when it is caused by a simple atomic event. But how do we know in a given case whether it is so caused? Or if he holds that it *must* be true because it *is* caused by such an event, I am compelled to ask how such is known to be the case. These comments are intended to indicate both that I hold a "correspondence (not coherence) theory of truth," and the sense in which I hold it—a sense which seems to me free from a fundamental difficulty that Mr. Russell's view of truth cannot get over or around. The event *to be* known is that which operates, on his own view, as cause of the proposition while it is also its verifier; although the proposition is the sole means of knowing the event! Such a view, like any strictly epistemological view, seems to me to assume a mysterious and inverifiable doctrine of pre-established harmony. How an event can be (i) what-is-to-be-known, hence by description is unknown, and (ii) what is capable of being *known* only through the medium of a proposition, which, in turn (iii) in order to be a case of knowledge or be true, must correspond to the to-be-known, is to me *the* epistemological miracle. For the doctrine states that a proposition is true when it conforms to that which is not known save through itself.

I should be happy to believe that what has been said is sufficiently definite and clear so that it is not necessary to say anything more on the subject. But there are criticisms of Mr. Russell's that I might seem to be evading were I to say nothing specifically about them. He asserts that he has several times asked me what the goal of inquiry is upon my theory, and has seen no answer to the question. A person turning to the Index of my *Logic: The Theory of Inquiry* will find the following heading: "Assertability, warranted, as end of inquiry." Some fourteen passages of the text are referred to. Unless there is a difference which escapes me between "end" and "goal," the following passage would seem to give the answer which Mr. Russell has missed:

"Moreover, inference, even in its connection with test, is not logically final and complete. The heart of the entire theory developed in this work is that the resolution of an indeterminate situation is the end, in the sense in which 'end' means *end-in-view* and in the sense which it means *close*."

The implication of the passage is that inquiry begins in an *indeterminate* situation, and not only begins in it but is controlled by its specific qualitative nature. Inquiry, as the set of operations by which the situation is resolved, has to discover and formulate the conditions that describe the problem in hand. For *they* are the conditions to be "satisfied" and the determinants of "success." Since these conditions are existential they can be determined only by observational operations. Upon a non-scientific level of inquiry, it is exhibited in the fact that we *look* and see; *listen* and hear; or in general terms that a motor as well as sensory factor is involved in any perceptual experience. The conditions discovered constitute the *conditions of the problem*; for data are always data of some specific problem and, hence are not given ready-made to an inquiry but are determined in and by it. Propositions about data are not cases of knowledge but the means of attaining it. When they are checked by reference to observed materials, they constitute the subject-matter of inferential *propositions*. The latter are means of attaining the goal of knowledge as warranted assertion, not instances or examples of knowledge.

If this statement is taken in its own terms, I think it will render unnecessary further comment on the notion Mr. Russell has ascribed to me, namely that "a belief is warranted, if as a tool, it is useful in some activity, i.e., if it is a cause of satisfaction of desire."

Mr. Russell observed: "Dr. Dewey *seems* to write as if a doubtful situation could exist without a personal doubter. I cannot think that he means this; he cannot intend to say, for example, that there were doubtful situations in astronomical and geological epochs before there was life."

When the term "doubtful situation" is taken in the meaning it possesses in the context of my general theory of experience, I *do* mean to say that it can exist without a personal doubter; and, moreover, that "personal states of doubt that are not evoked by, and are not relative to, some existential situation are pathological.... The habit of disposing of the doubtful as if it belonged only to *us* rather than to the existential situation in which we are caught and implicated is an inheritance from subjectivistic psychology." (*Logic*, p.106.)

As far as cosmological speculation on the indeterminate situations in astronomical and geological epochs is relevant to my theory, *any* view which holds that man is a part of nature, not outside it, will hold that this fact of being part of nature qualifies his "experience" throughout. Hence the view will certainly hold that indeterminacy in human experience is evidence of some corresponding indeterminacy in the processes of nature within which man exists (acts) and out of which he arose.

I do not wish to conclude without saying that I have tried to conduct my discussion in the spirit indicated by Mr. Russell. In this process I am aware of the acute bearing of his remark that "it is because the difference goes deep that it is difficult to find words which both sides can accept as a fair statement of the issue." In view of the depth of the difference, I can hardly hope to have succeeded completely in overcoming this difficulty. But at least I have been more concerned to make my own position intelligible than to refute Mr. Russell's view, so that the controversial remarks I have made have their source in the belief that definite contrast are important, perhaps indispensable, means of making any view sharp in outline and definite in content.

VII

Russell on Religion

My own view on religion is that of Lucretius. I regard it as a disease born of fear and as a source of untold misery to the human race. I cannot, however, deny that it has made some contributions to civilization. It helped in early days to fix the calendar, and it caused Egyptian priests to chronicle eclipses with such care that in time they became able to predict them. These two services I am prepared to acknowledge, but I do not know of any others.

The word *religion* is used nowadays in a very loose sense. Some people, under the influence of extreme Protestantism, employ the word to denote any serious personal convictions as to morals or the nature of the universe. Religion is primarily a social phenomenon. Churches may owe their origin to teachers with strong individual convictions, but these teachers have

75

seldom had much influence upon the churches that they founded, whereas churches have had enormous influence upon the communities in which they flourished. To take the case that is of most interest to members of Western civilization: The teaching of Christ, as it appears in the Gospels, has had extraordinarily little to do with the ethics of Christians. The most important thing about Christianity, from a social and historical point of view, is not Christ, but the church, and if we are to judge of Christianity as a social force, we must not go to the Gospels for our material. Christ taught that you should not fight, that you should not go to church, and that you should not punish adultery. Neither Catholics not Protestants have shown any strong desire to follow His teaching in any of these respects. Some of the Franciscans, it is true, attempted to teach the doctrine of apostolic poverty, but the Pope condemned them, and their doctrine was declared heretical. Or again, consider such a text as "Judge not, that ye be not judged," and ask yourself what influence such a text has had upon the Inquisition and the Ku Klux Klan.

There is nothing accidental about this difference between a church and its founder. As soon as absolute truth is supposed to be contained in the sayings of a certain man, there is a body of experts to interpret his sayings, and these experts infallibly acquire power, since they hold the key to truth. Like any other privileged caste, they use their power for their own advantage. They are, however, in one respect worse than any other privileged caste, since it is their business to expound an unchanging truth, revealed once for all in utter perfection, so they become necessarily opponents of all intellectual and moral progress. The church opposed Galileo and Darwin; in our own day it opposes Freud. Pope Gregory the Great wrote to a certain bishop a letter beginning: "A report has reached us which we cannot mention without a blush, that thou expoundest grammar to certain friends." The bishop was compelled by pontifical authority to desist from this wicked labor and Latinity did not recover until the Renaissance. It is not only intellectually but also morally that religion is pernicious. I mean by this that it teaches ethical codes which are not conducive to human happiness. The churches opposed the abolition of slavery as long as they dared, and with a few well-advertised exceptions they oppose at the present day every movement toward economic justice. The Pope has officially condemned Socialism.

The worst feature of the Christian religion, however, is its attitude toward sex—an attitude so morbid and so unnatural that it can be understood only when taken in relation to the sickness of the civilized world at the time the Roman Empire was decaying. We sometimes hear talk to the effect that Christianity improved the status of women. This is one of the grossest perversions of history that is possible to make. Women cannot enjoy a tolerable position in society where it is considered of the utmost importance that they should not infringe a very rigid moral code.

Monks have always regarded Woman primarily as the temptress; they have thought of her mainly as the inspirer of impure lusts. The teaching of the church has been, and still is, that virginity is best, but that for those who find this impossible marriage is permissible. "It is better to marry than to burn," as St. Paul brutally puts it. By making marriage indissoluble, and by stamping out all knowledge of the *ars amandi* (art of loving), the church did what it could to secure that the only form of sex which it permitted should involve very little pleasure and a great deal of pain. The opposition to birth control has, in fact, the same motive: If a woman has a child a year until she dies worn out, it is not to be supposed that she will derive much pleasure from her married life; therefore birth control must be discouraged.

The conception of Sin which is bound up with Christian ethics is one that does an extraordinary amount of harm, since it affords people an outlet for their sadism which they believe to be legitimate, and even noble. Take, for example, the question of the prevention of syphilis. It is known that, by precautions taken in advance, the danger of contracting this disease can be made negligible. Christians, however, object to the dissemination of knowledge of this fact, since they hold it good that sinners should be punished. They hold this so good that they are even willing that punishment should extend to the wives and children of sinners. There are in the world at the present moment many thousands of children suffering from congenital syphilis who would never have been born but for the desire of Christians to see sinners punished. I cannot understand how doctrines leading to this fiendish cruelty can be considered to have any good effects upon morals.

It is not only in regard to sexual behavior but also in regard to knowledge on sex subjects that the attitude of Christians is dangerous to human welfare. I do not think there can be any defense for the view that knowledge is ever undesirable. Almost every adult in a Christian community is more or less diseased nervously as a result of the taboo on sex knowledge when he or she was young. And the sense of sin which is thus artificially implanted is one of the causes of cruelty, timidity, and stupidity in later life. There is no rational ground of any sort or kind for keeping a child ignorant of anything that he may wish to know, whether on sex or any other matter. And we shall never get a sane population until this fact is recognized in early education, which is impossible so long as the churches are able to control educational politics.

The objections to religion are of two sorts—intellectual and moral. The intellectual objection is that there is no reason to suppose any religion true; the moral objection is that religious precepts date from a time when men were more cruel than they are and therefore tend to perpetuate inhumanities which the moral conscience of the age would otherwise outgrow.

To take the intellectual objection first: There is a certain tendency in our practical age to consider that it does not much matter whether religious teaching is true or not, since the important question is whether it is useful. The usual argument of religious people on this subject is roughly as follows: "I and my friends are persons of amazing intelligence and virtue. It is hardly conceivable that so much intelligence and virtue could have come about by chance. There must, therefore, be someone at least as intelligent and virtuous as we are who set the cosmic machinery in motion with a view to producing Us." I am sorry to say that I do not find this argument so impressive as it is found by those who use it.

Considered as the climax to a vast process, we do not really seem to me sufficiently marvelous. Of course, I am aware that many divines are far more marvelous than I am, and that I cannot wholly appreciate merits so far transcending my own. Nevertheless, even after making allowances under this head, I cannot but think that Omnipotence operating through all eternity might have produced something better. And then we have to remember that even this result is only a flash in the pan. The earth will not always remain habitable. The second law of thermodynamics makes it scarcely possible to doubt that the universe is running down, and that ultimately nothing of the slightest interest will be possible anywhere. Of course, it is open to us to say that when that time comes God will wind up the machinery again; but if we do say this, we can base our evidence only upon faith, not upon one shred of scientific evidence. So far as scientific evidence goes, the universe has crawled by slow stages to a somewhat pitiful result on this earth and is going to crawl by still more pitiful stages to a condition of universal death. If this is to be taken as evidence of purpose, I can only say that the purpose is one that does not appeal to me.

The Christian emphasis on the individual soul has had a profound influence upon the ethics of the Christian community. It is a doctrine fundamentally akin to that of the Stoics, arising as theirs did in communities that could no longer cherish political hopes. The early Christians had a conception

of personal holiness as something quite independent of benefi-
cent action, since holiness had to be something that could be
achieved by people who were impotent in action. Social virtue
came therefore to be excluded from Christian ethics. To this
day conventional Christians think an adulterer more wicked
than a politician who takes bribes, although the latter probably does a thousand times as much harm.

Their individualism culminated in the doctrine of the
immortality of the individual soul, which was to enjoy hereaf-
ter endless bliss or endless woe, according to circumstances.
The circumstances upon which this momentous difference
depended were somewhat curious. For example, if you died
immediately after a priest had sprinkled water upon you while
pronouncing certain words, you inherited eternal bliss: whereas if after a long and virtuous life you happened to be struck
by lightning at a moment when you were using bad language
because you had broken a bootlace, you would inherit eternal
torment. The Spaniards in Mexico and Peru used to baptize
Indian infants and then immediately dash their brains out: By
this means they secured that these infants went to Heaven. No
orthodox Christian can find any logical reason for condemn-
ing their action. In countless ways the doctrine of personal
immortality in its Christian form has had disastrous effects
upon morals.

To judge of the moral influence of any institution upon a
community, we have to consider the kind of impulse which is
embodied in the institution. Sometimes the impulse concerned
is quite obvious, sometimes it is more hidden. An Alpine club,
for example, obviously embodies the impulse to adventure,
and a learned society the impulse toward knowledge. The
family as an institution embodies jealousy and parental feeling; a football club or a political party embodies the impulse
toward competitive play; but the two greatest institutions—
namely the church and the state—are more complex in their
psychological motivation. The primary purpose of the state is

clearly security against both internal criminals and external enemies. It is rooted in the tendency of children to huddle together when they are frightened and to look for a grownup person who will give them a sense of security. Undoubtedly the most important source of religion is fear; this can be seen in the present day, since anything that causes alarm is apt to turn people's thoughts to God. Battle, pestilence, and shipwreck all tend to make people religious. Religion has, however, other appeals besides that of terror; it appeals especially to our human self-esteem. If Christianity is true, mankind are not such pitiful worms as they seem to be; they are of interest to the Creator of the universe, who takes the trouble to be pleased with them when they behave well and displeased when they behave badly. This is a great compliment. We should not think of studying an ants' nest to find out which of the ants performed their formicular duty, and we should certainly not think of picking out those individual ants who were remiss and putting them into a bonfire. If God does this for us, it is a compliment to our importance; and it is even a pleasanter compliment if he awards to the good among us everlasting happiness in heaven.

The idea is that we should all be wicked if we did not hold to the Christian religion. It seems to me that the people who have held to it have been for the most part extremely wicked. You find this curious fact, that the more intense has been the religion of any period and the more profound has been the dogmatic belief, the greater has been the cruelty and the worse has been the state of affairs. In the so-called ages of faith, when men really did believe the Christian religion in all its completeness, there was the Inquisition with its tortures; there were millions of unfortunate women burned as witches; and there was every kind of cruelty practiced upon all sorts of people in the name of religion.

It would seem, therefore, that the impulses embodied in religion are fear, conceit, and hatred. The purpose of religion, one may say, is to give an air of respectability to these passions, provided they run in certain channels. It is because these passions make, on the whole, for human misery that religion is a force for evil, since it permits men to indulge these passions without restraint.

I can imagine at this point an objection worthy to be examined. Hatred and fear, it may be said, are essential human characteristics; mankind always has felt them and always will. The best that you can do with them, I may be told, is to direct them into certain channels in which they are less harmful than they would be in certain other channels. A Christian theologian might say that their treatment by the church is analogous to its treatment of the sex impulse, which it deplores. It attempts to render concupiscence innocuous by confining it within the bounds of matrimony. So it may be said, if mankind must inevitably feel hatred, it is better to direct this hatred against those who are really harmful, and this is precisely what the church does by its conception of righteousness.

The church's conception of righteousness is socially undesirable in various ways—first and foremost in its depreciation of intelligence and science. The second and more fundamental objection to the utilization of fear and hatred in the way practiced by the church is that these emotions can now be almost wholly eliminated from human nature by educational, economic, and political reforms. An education designed to eliminate fear is by no means difficult to create. It is only necessary to treat a child with kindness, to put him in an environment where initiative is possible without disastrous results, and to save him from contact with adults who have irrational terrors, whether of the dark, of mice, or of social revolution.

Religion is based, I think, primarily and mainly upon fear. Fear is the basis of the whole thing—fear of the mysterious, fear of defeat, fear of death. Fear is the parent of cruelty, and therefore it is no wonder if cruelty and religion have gone hand in hand.

You find as you look around the world that every single bit of progress in humane feeling, every improvement in the criminal law, every step toward the diminution of war, every step toward better treatment of the colored races, or every mitigation of slavery, every moral progress that there has been in the world has been consistently opposed by the organized churches of the world. I say quite deliberately that the Christian religion, as organized in its churches, has been and still is the principal enemy of moral progress in the world.

The whole conception of God is a conception derived from the ancient Oriental despotisms. It is a conception quite unworthy of free men. When you hear people in church debasing themselves and saying they are miserable sinners, and all the rest of it, it seems contemptible and not worthy of self-respecting human beings.

The injustice, the cruelty, and the misery that exist in the modern world are an inheritance from the past, and their ultimate source is economic since life-and-death competition for the means of subsistence was in former days inevitable. It is not inevitable in our age. With our present industrial technique we can, if we choose, provide a tolerable subsistence for everybody. We could also secure that the world's population should be stationary if we were not prevented by the political influences of churches which prefer war, pestilence, and famine to contraception. The knowledge exists by which universal happiness can be secured; the chief obstacle to its utilization for that purpose is the teaching of religion. Religion prevents our children from having a rational education; religion prevents us from removing the fundamental causes of war; religion prevents us from teaching the ethic of scientific cooperation in place of the old fierce doctrines of sin and punishment.

We ought to make the best we can of the world. A good

world needs knowledge, kindliness, and courage; it does not need a regretful hankering after the past of a fettering of the free intelligence by the words uttered long ago by ignorant men. It needs a fearless outlook and a free intelligence. It needs hope for the future, not looking back all the time toward a past that is dead, which we trust will be far surpassed by the future that our intelligence can create.

VIII

Dewey on Religion

Never before in history has mankind been so much of two minds, so divided into two camps, as it is today. Religions have traditionally been allied with ideas of the supernatural, and often have been based upon explicit beliefs about it. Today there are many who hold that nothing worthy of being called religious is possible apart from the supernatural. They agree in one point: the necessity for a Supernatural Being and for an immortality that is beyond the power of nature.

The opposed group consists of those who think the advance of culture and science has completely discredited the supernatural and with it all religions that were allied with belief in it.

There is one idea held in common by these two opposite groups: identification of the religious with the supernatural. I shall question the grounds for this identification and develop another conception of the nature of the religious phase of experience that separates it from the supernatural so that what is genuinely religious will undergo an emancipation; so that then, for the first time, the religious aspect of experience will be free to develop freely on its own account. The heart of my point is that there is a difference between religion and the religious; between anything that may be denoted by a noun substantive and the quality of experience that is designated by an adjective.

The logic involved in getting rid of inconvenient aspects of past religions compels us to inquire how much in religions now accepted are survivals from outgrown cultures. It demands that in imagination we wipe the slate clean and start afresh by asking what would be the idea of the unseen, of the manner of its control over us and the ways in which reverence and obedience would be manifested, if whatever is basically religious in experience had the opportunity to express itself free from all historic encumbrances.

There is no such thing as religion in the singular. There is only a multitude of religions. "Religion" is strictly a collective term. I am not proposing a religion but rather the emancipation of elements and outlooks that may be called religious.

I can illustrate what I mean by a common phenomenon in contemporary life. It is widely supposed that a person who does not accept any religion is thereby shown to be a non-religious person. Yet it is conceivable that religions now prevent, because of the weight of historic incumbrances, the religious quality of experience from coming to consciousness and finding the expression that is appropriate to present conditions, intellectual and moral. I believe many persons are so repelled from what exists as a religion by its intellectual and moral implications, that they are not even aware of attitudes in themselves that if they came to fruition would be genuinely religious. I hope this remark may help make clear what I mean by the distinction between "religion" as a noun substantive and "religious" as adjectival.

Religious does not denote anything that can exist by itself or that can be organized into a particular and distinctive form of existence. It denotes attitudes that may be taken toward every object and every proposed end or ideal. It is the polar opposite of some type of experience that can exist by itself. "Religious" as a quality of experience signifies something that may belong to all experiences as aesthetic, scientific, moral, political. The actual religious quality is the *effect* produced, the better adjustment in life and its conditions. If reorientation actually occurs, it and the sense of security and stability accompanying it are forces on their own account. It takes place in different persons in a multitude of ways. It is sometimes brought about by devotion to a cause; sometimes by a passage of poetry that opens a new perspective; sometimes as was the case with Spinoza—deemed an atheist in his day—through philosophical reflection.

It is the claim of religions that they effect this generic and enduring change in attitude. I should like to turn the statement around and say that whenever this change takes place there is a definitely religious attitude, a religious outlook and function.

There can be no doubt of our dependence upon forces beyond our control. That human destiny is so interwoven with forces beyond human control renders it unnecessary to suppose that dependence and the humility that accompanies it have to find the particular channel that is prescribed by traditional doctrines. What is especially significant is rather the form which the sense of dependence takes. Fear never gave stable perspective in the life of anyone. For our dependence is manifested in those relations to the environment that support our undertakings and aspirations as much as it is in the defeats inflicted upon us. The essentially unreligious attitude is that which attributes human achievement and purpose to man in isolation from the world of physical nature and his fellows. Our successes are dependent upon the cooperation of nature. The sense of the dignity of human nature is as religious as is the sense of awe and reverence as a cooperating part of a larger whole. Natural piety is not of necessity either a fatalistic acquiescence in natural happenings or a romantic idealization of the world. It may rest upon a just sense of nature as the whole of which we are parts, while it also recognizes that we are parts that are marked by intelligence and purpose, having the capacity to strive by their aid to bring conditions into a greater consonance with what is humanly desirable.

Understanding and knowledge also enter into a perspective that is religious in quality. Faith in the continued disclosing of truth through directed cooperative human endeavor is more religious in quality than is any faith in a completed revelation.

Any activity pursued in behalf of an ideal end against obstacles and in spite of threats of personal loss because of conviction of its general and enduring value is religious in quality. Many a person—men and women in the humblest walks of life have achieved, without presumption and without display, such unification of themselves and of their relations to the conditions of existence. If I have said anything about religious and religion that seems harsh, I have said those things because of a firm belief that the claim on the part of religions to possess a monopoly of ideals and of the supernatural means by which alone, it is alleged, they can be furthered, stands in the way of the realization of distinctively religious values inherent in natural experience.

Apologists for a religion often point to the shift that goes on in scientific ideas and materials as evidence of the unreliability of science as a mode of knowledge. But in fact they miss the point. Science is not constituted by any particular body of subject-matter. It is constituted by a method, a method of changing beliefs by means of tested inquiry. It is its glory, not its condemnation, that its subject-matter develops as the method is improved.

The idea of God is one of ideal possibilities unified through imaginative realization and projection. But this idea of God, or of the divine, is connected with all the natural forces and conditions—including man and human association—that promote the growth of the ideal and that further its realization. We are in the presence neither of ideals completely embodied in existence nor yet of ideals that are mere rootless ideals, fantasies, utopias. For there are forces in nature and society that generate and support the ideals. They are further unified by the action that gives them coherence and solidity. It is this *active* relation between ideal and actual to which I would give the name "God."

There exist concretely and experimentally goods—the value of art in all its forms, of knowledge, of effort and of rest after striving, of education and fellowship, of friendship and love, of growth in mind and body. These goods are there and yet they are relatively embryonic. Many persons are shut out from generous participation in them; there are forces at work that threaten and sap existent goods as well as prevent their expansion. A clear and intense conception of a union of ideal ends with actual conditions is capable of arousing steady emotion. It may be fed by every experience, no matter what its material.

The *function* of such a working union of the ideal and actual seems to me to be identical with the force that has in fact been attached to the conception of God in all the religions that have a spiritual content; and a clear idea of that function seems to me urgently needed at the present time.

The reality of ideal ends and values in their authority over us is an undoubted fact. The validity of justice, affection, and that intellectual correspondence of our ideas with realities that we call truth, is so assured in its hold upon humanity that it is unnecessary for the religious attitude to encumber itself with the apparatus of dogma and doctrine.

We are involved in all the problems of the existence of evil that have haunted theology in the past and that the most ingenious apologetics have not faced, much less met. The significance of ideal ends and meanings is, indeed, closely connected with the fact that there are in life all sorts of things that are evil to us, because we would have them otherwise. Were existing conditions wholly good the notion of possibilities to be realized would never emerge.

Belief in a sudden and complete transmutation through conversion and in the objective efficacy of prayer, is too easy a way out of difficulties. It leaves matters in general just about as they were before; that is, sufficiently bad so that there is additional support for the idea that only supernatural aid can better them. The position of natural intelligence is that there exists a *mixture* of good and evil, and that reconstruction in the direction of the good which is indicated by ideal ends, must take place, if at all, through continued cooperative effort. There is at least enough impulse toward justice, kindliness, and order so that if it were mobilized for action the disorder, cruelty, and oppression that exist would be reduced.

I would remind you it is the intellectual side of the religious attitude that I have been considering. The crisis today as to the intellectual content of religious belief has been caused by the change in the intellectual climate due to the increase of our knowledge and our means of understanding. I have tried to show that this change is not fatal to the religious values in our common experience, however adverse its impact may be upon historic religions. Rather, provided that the methods and results of intelligence at work are frankly adopted, the change is liberating.

It clarifies our ideals, rendering them less subject to illusion and fantasy. The change gives aspiration for natural knowledge a definitely religious character, since growth in understanding of nature is seen to be organically related to the formation of ideal ends.

All purpose is selective, and all intelligent action includes deliberate choice. In the degree in which we cease to depend upon belief in the supernatural, selection is enlightened and choice can be made in behalf of ideals whose inherent relations to conditions and consequences are understood. Were the naturalistic foundations and bearings of religion grasped, the religious element in life would emerge. Religion would then be found to have its natural place in every aspect of human experience that is concerned with estimate, of possibilities, with emotional stir by possibilities as yet unrealized, and with all action in behalf of their realization. All that is significant in human experience falls within this frame.

It is impossible to ignore the fact that historic Christianity has been committed to a separation of sheep and goats; the saved and the lost; the elect and the mass. Spiritual aristocracy, as well as *laissez-faire* with respect to natural and human intervention, is deeply embedded in its tradition. Lip service has been given to the idea of the common brotherhood of all men. But those outside the fold of the church and those who do not rely upon belief in the supernatural have been regarded as only potential brothers, still requiring adoption into the family. I cannot understand how any realization of the democratic ideal as a vital moral and spiritual ideal in human affairs is possible without surrender of the conception of the basic division to which supernatural Christianity is committed. Whether or not we are, save in some metaphorical sense, all brothers, we are at least all in the same boat traversing the same turbulent ocean. The potential religious significance of this fact is infinite.

IX

Russell—Envoi

There is only too much reason to fear that Western civilization, if not the whole world, is likely in the near future to go
through a period during which, if we are not careful to
remember them, the things that we are attempting to preserve
may be forgotten in bitterness and poverty and disaster. Courage, hope and unshakable conviction will be necessary if we are
to emerge from the dark time spiritually undamaged. It is
worth while, before the actual danger is upon us, to collect our
thoughts, to marshal our hopes, and to plant in our hearts a
firm belief in our ideals.

It is not the first time that such disasters have threatened the
Western world. The fall of Rome was another such time, and in
that time, as now, varying moods of despair, escape and robust
faith were exemplified in the writings of leading men. What

emerged and became the kernel of the new civilization was the Christian church.

The sages of our time have a similar duty to perform. It is their duty to posterity to crystallize the achievements, the hopes, and the ideals which have made our time great, to study them with monumental simplicity, so they may shine like a beacon light through the coming darkness.

Two very different conceptions of human life are struggling for mastery of the world. In the West, we see man's greatness in the individual life. A great society for us is one which is composed of individuals who, as far as is humanly possible, are happy, free, and creative. The State for us is a convenience, not an object of worship.

The Russian Government has a different conception of the ends of life. The individual is thought of no importance: He is expendable. What is important is the State, which is regarded as something almost divine and having a welfare of its own not consisting in the welfare of citizens. This view, which Marx took over from Hegel, is fundamentally opposed to the Christian ethic, which in the West is accepted by free-thinkers as much as by Christians. In the Soviet world human dignity counts for nothing.

It is this conception that we have to fight, a conception which to my mind and to that of most men who appreciate what the Western world stands for, would, if it prevailed, take everything out of life that gives it value. I cannot imagine a greater or more profound cause for which to fight. But if we are to win a victory—not only on the battlefield but in the hearts of men and in the institutions that they support—we must be clear in our own minds as to what it is that we value, and we must fortify our courage against the threat of adversity.

The first step in wisdom, as well as in morality, is to open the windows of the ego as wide as possible. Most people find little difficulty in including their children within the compass of their desires. In slightly lesser degree they include their friends, and in time of danger their country. But it is not enough to enlarge our sympathies to embrace our own country. If the world is ever to have peace it will be necessary to learn to embrace the whole human race.

Few things are more purifying to our conception of values than to contemplate the gradual rise of man from his obscure and difficult beginnings to his present eminence. Man, when he first emerged was a rare and hunted species, not so fleet as the deer, not so nimble as the monkey, unable to defend himself against wild beasts, without the protection of warm fur against rain and cold, living precariously upon the food that he could gather, without weapons, without domestic animals, without agriculture.

The one advantage that he possessed—intelligence—gave him security. He learned the use of fire, of bows and arrows, of language, of domestic animals and, at last, agriculture. He learned to cooperate in communities, to build great palaces and pyramids, to explore the world in all directions and, at last, to cope with disease and poverty. He studied the stars, he invented geometry, and he learned to substitute machines for muscles in necessary labor. Some of the most important of these advances are very recent and are as yet confined to Western nations.

In former days most children died in infancy, mortality in adult life was very high, and in every country the great majority of the population endured abject poverty. Now certain nations have succeeded in preserving the lives of the overwhelming majority of infants, in lowering enormously the adult death rate, and in nearly eliminating abject poverty. Other nations, where disease and abject poverty are still the rule, could achieve the same level of well-being by adopting the same methods. There is, therefore, a new hope for mankind.

The hope cannot be realized unless the causes of present evils are understood. But it is the hope that needs to be emphasized. Modern man is master of his fate. What he suffers he suffers because it is nature's decree. Happiness is his if he will adopt the means that lie ready to his hands.

We of the Western world, faced with Communism's hostile criticism, have been too modest and too defensive in our attitude. Throughout the long ages since life began the mechanism of evolution has involved cruel suffering, endless struggle for bare subsistence, and in the end, in most cases, death by starvation. This is the law in the animal kingdom, and it remained, until the present century, the law among human beings also. Now, at last, certain nations have discovered how to prevent abject poverty, how to prevent the pain and sorrow and waste of useless births, condemned to premature death, and how to substitute intelligence and care for the blind ruthlessness of nature.

The nations that have made this discovery are trustees for the future of mankind. They must have the courage of their new way of life and not allow themselves to be bemused or bewildered by the slogans of the semi-civilized. We have a right to hopes that are rational, that can be itemized and set forth in statistics. If we allow ourselves to be robbed of these hopes for the sake of irrational dreams, we shall be traitors to the human race.

If bad times lie ahead of us, we should remember while they last the slow march of man, checkered in the past by devastations and retrogressions, but always resuming the movement towards progress. Spinoza, who was one of the wisest of men and who lived consistently in accordance with his own wisdom, advised men to view passing events "under the aspect of eternity." Those who can learn to do this will find a painful present much more bearable than it would otherwise be. They can see it as a passing moment—a discord to be resolved, a tunnel to be traversed. The small child who has hurt himself weeps as if the world contained nothing but sorrow, because his mind is confined to the present. A man who has learned wisdom from Spinoza can see even a lifetime of suffering as a passing moment in the life of humanity. And the human race itself from its obscure beginning to its unknown end, is only a minute episode in the life of the universe.

With increase of wisdom our thoughts acquire a wider scope both in space and in time. The child lives in the minute, the boy in the day, the instinctive man in the year. The man imbued with history lives in the epoch. Spinoza would have us live not in the minute, the day, the year or the epoch but in eternity. Those who learn to do this will find that it takes away the frantic quality of misfortune and prevents the trend towards madness that comes with overwhelming disaster. He spent the last day of his life telling cheerful anecdotes to his host. He had written: "The wise man thinks less about death than about anything else," and he carried out this precept when it came to his own death.

I do not mean that the wise man will be destitute of emotion—on the contrary, he will feel friendship, benevolence, and compassion in a higher degree than the man who has not emancipated himself from personal anxieties. His ego will not be a wall between him and the rest of mankind. He will feel, like Buddha, that he cannot be completely happy while anyone is miserable. He will feel pain—a wider and more diffused pain than that of the egoist—but he will not find the pain unendurable. He will not lose poise and self control. Like Milton's Satan he will say:

The mind is its own place, and in itself.
Can make a Heav'n of Hell, a Hell of Heav'n.

Above all he will remember that each generation is a trustee to future generations of the mental and moral treasure that man has accumulated through the ages. It is easy to forget the glory of man.

This is half of the truth. The other half is uttered by Hamlet: "What a piece of work is a man! how noble in reason! how infinite in faculty! In form and moving how express and admirable! in action how like an angel! in apprehension how like a god!"

Soviet man crawling on his knees to betray his friends and family to slow butchery, is hardly worthy of Hamlet's words, but it is possible to be worthy of them. It is possible for every one of us. Each one of us can enlarge his mind, release his imagination, and spread wide his affection and benevolence. And it is those who do this whom ultimately mankind reveres. The East reveres Buddha, the West reveres Christ. Both taught love as the secret of wisdom.

Those who live nobly, even if in their day they live obscurely, need not fear that they will have lived in vain. Something radiates from their lives, some light that shows the way to their friends, their neighbors—perhaps to long future ages. I find many men nowadays oppressed with a sense of impotence, with a feeling that in the vastness of modern societies there is nothing of importance that the individual can do. This is a mistake. The individual, if he is filled with love of mankind, with breadth of vision, with courage and with endurance, can do a great deal.

In spite of some alarmists, it is hardly likely that our species will completely exterminate itself. And so long as man continues to exist, we may be pretty sure that, whatever he may suffer for a time, and whatever brightness may be eclipsed, he will emerge sooner or later, perhaps strengthened and reinvigorated by a period of mental sleep. The universe is vast and men are but tiny specks on an insignificant planet. But the more we realize our minuteness and our impotence in the face of cosmic forces, the more astonishing becomes what human beings have achieved.

It is to the possible achievements of man that our ultimate loyalty is due, and in that thought the brief troubles of our unquiet epoch become endurable. Much wisdom remains to be learned, and if it is only to be learned through adversity, we must endeavor to endure adversity with what fortitude we can command. But if we can acquire wisdom soon enough, adversity may not be necessary and the future of man may be happier than any part of his past.

X

Dewey—Envoi

As I conclude, I am aware how largely controversy has bulked in my replies. In any case, it is congenial to believe that conflict of ideas, as distinct from that of force, is a necessary condition of advance in understanding, and that agreements which exist only because of lack of critical contact and comparison are superficial. Discussion is communication, and it is by communication that ideas are shared and become a common possession. It is less important that we all believe alike than that we all alike inquire freely and put at the disposal of one another such glimpses as we may obtain of the truth for which we are in search.

During the period of my lifetime (I do not attempt to conceal the fact that I have managed to exist eighty years) events of the utmost significance have taken place in this country, a period that covers more than half of its life in its present form. Not all the country was in a pioneer state eighty years ago, but it was still so close that the traditions of the pioneer were active agencies in forming the thoughts and shaping the beliefs of those who were born into its life. It was a country of physical opportunity and invitation. There was in existence a group of men who were capable of re-adapting older institutions and ideas to meet the situations provided by new physical conditions—a group of men extraordinarily gifted in political inventiveness.

At the present time, the frontier is moral, not physical. Unused resources are now human rather than material. They are found in the waste of grown men and women who are without the chance to work, and in the young men and young women who find doors closed where there was once opportunity.

This is what I mean when I say that we now have to recreate by deliberate and determined endeavor the kind of democracy which in its origin one hundred and fifty years ago was largely the product of a fortunate combination of men and circumstances. As a way of life, democracy signifies the possession and continual use of certain attitudes, forming personal character and determining desire and purpose in all the relations of life.

Democracy as a personal, an individual, way of life involves nothing fundamentally new. But when applied it puts a new practical meaning in old ideas. Put into effect it signifies that powerful present enemies of democracy can be successfully met only by the creation of personal attitudes in individual human beings; that we must get over our tendency to think that its defense can be found in any external means whatever, whether military or civil, if they are separated from individual attitudes so deep-seated as to constitute personal character.

Democracy is a way of life controlled by a working faith in the possibilities of human nature. Belief in the Common Man is a familiar article in the democratic creed. That belief is without basis and significance save as it means faith in the potentialities of human nature as that nature is exhibited in every human being irrespective of race, color, sex, birth and family, of material or cultural wealth. This faith may be enacted in statutes, but it is only on paper unless it is put in force in the attitudes which human beings display to one another in all the incidents and relations of daily life. To denounce Naziism for intolerance, cruelty and stimulation of hatred amounts to fostering insincerity if, in our personal relations to other persons, if in our daily walk and conversation, we are moved by racial, color, or other class prejudice; indeed by anything save a generous belief in their possibilities as human beings, a belief which brings with it the need for providing conditions which will enable these capacities to reach fulfillment. The democratic faith in human equality is belief that every human being has the right to equal opportunity with every other person for development of whatever gifts he has. It is belief in the capacity of every person to lead his own life free from coercion and imposition by others.

Democracy is a way of personal life controlled not merely by faith in human nature in general but by faith in the capacity of human beings for intelligent judgment and action if proper conditions are furnished. I have been accused more than once and from opposed quarters of an undue, a utopian, faith in the possibilities of intelligence and in education as a correlate of intelligence. At all events I did not invent this faith. I acquired it from my surroundings as far as these surroundings were animated by the democratic spirit. For what is the faith of democracy in the role of consultation, of conference, of persuasion, of discussion in formation of public opinion, which in the long run is self-corrective, except faith in the capacity of the intelligence of the common man to respond with common sense to the free play of facts and ideas which are secured by effective guarantees of free inquiry, free association, and free communication? I am willing to leave to upholders of totalitarian states of the right and the left the view that faith in the capacities of intelligence is utopian. For the faith is so deeply embedded in the methods which are intrinsic to democracy that when a professed democrat denies the faith he convicts himself of treachery to his profession.

When I think of the conditions under which men and women are living in many foreign countries today, fear of espionage, with danger hanging over the meeting of friends for friendly conversation in private gatherings, I am inclined to believe that the heart and final guarantee of democracy is in free gatherings of neighbors on the street corner to discuss back and forth what is read in uncensored news of the day, and in the gatherings of friends in the living rooms of houses and apartments to converse freely with one another. Intolerance, abuse, calling of names because of differences of opinion about religion or politics or business, as well as because of differences of race, color, wealth, or degree of culture, are treason to the democratic way of life. For everything which bars freedom and fullness of communication sets up barriers that divide human beings into sets and cliques, into antagonistic sects and factions, and thereby undermines the democratic way of life. Merely legal guarantees of the civil liberties of free belief, free expression, free assembly are of little avail if in daily life freedom of communication, the give and take of ideas, facts, experiences, is choked by mutual suspicion, by abuse, by fear, and hatred. These things destroy the essential condition of the democratic way of living even more effectually than open coercion, which—as the example of totalitarian states proves—is effective only when it succeeds in breeding hate, suspicion, intolerance in the minds of individual human beings.

Finally democracy as a way of life is controlled by personal faith in personal day-by-day working together with others. Democracy is the belief that even when needs and ends or consequences are different for each individual, the habit of amicable cooperation—which may include, as in sport, rivalry and competition—is itself a priceless addition to life. To take as far as possible every conflict which arises—and they are bound to arise—out of the atmosphere and medium of force, of violence as a means of settlement, into that of discussion and of intelligence, is to treat those who disagree—even profoundly—with us as those from whom we may learn, and in so far, as friends. A genuinely democratic faith in peace is faith in the possibility of conducting disputes, controversies, and conflicts as cooperative undertakings in which both parties learn by giving the other a chance to express itself, instead of having one party conquer by forceful suppression of the other—a suppression which is none the less one of violence when it takes place by psychological means of ridicule, abuse, intimidation, instead of by overt imprisonment or in concentration camps. To cooperate by giving differences a chance to show themselves because of the belief that the expression of difference is not only a right of the other persons but is a means of enriching one's own life-experience, is inherent in the democratic personal way of life.

If what has been said is charged with being a set of moral commonplaces, my only reply is that that is just the point of saying them. For to get rid of the habit of thinking of democracy as something institutional and external and to acquire the habit of treating it as a way of personal life is to realize that democracy is a reality only as it is indeed a commonplace of living.

Since my adult years have been given to the pursuit of philosophy, I shall ask your indulgence if in concluding I state briefly the democratic faith in the formal terms of a philosophic position. So stated, democracy is belief in the ability of human experience to generate the aims and methods by which further experience will grow in ordered richness. Every other form of moral and social faith rests upon the idea that experience must be subjected to some form of external control; to some "authority" alleged to exist outside the process of experience. Democracy is the faith that the process of experience is more important than any special result attained, so that special results achieved are of ultimate value only as they are used to enrich and order the ongoing process. Faith in democracy is all one with faith in experience and education.

Knowledge of conditions as they are is the only solid ground for communication and sharing; all other communication means the subjection of some persons to the personal opinion of other persons. Need and desire—out of which grow purpose and direction of energy—go beyond what exists, and hence beyond knowledge, beyond science. They continually open the way into the unexplored and unattained future.

Democracy as compared with other ways of life is the sole way of living which believes wholeheartedly in the process of experience as end and as means; as that which is capable of generating the science which is the sole dependable authority for the direction of further experience and which releases emotions, needs, and desires so as to call into being the things that have not existed in the past. For every way of life that fails in its democracy limits the contacts, the exchanges, the communications, the interactions by which experience is steadied while it is also enlarged and enriched. The task of this release and enrichment is one that has to be carried on day by day. Since it is one that can have no end till experience itself comes to an end, the task of democracy is forever that of creation of a freer and more humane experience in which all share and to which all contribute.

Notes

Editor's Preface

1. *Dialogue on John Dewey*, ed. Corliss Lamont, (New York: Horizon Press, 1959), p. 35.
2. Bertrand Russell, *A History of Western Philosophy* (New York: Simon and Schuster, 1945), p. 812.
3. Bertrand Russell, *The Philosophy of Logical Atomism*, R.C. Marsh, ed., (London: Macmillan, 1956), p. 270.
4. John Dewey, *Experience and Nature* (Chicago: Open Court Publishing Company, 1925), p. 57.
5. Ibid., p. 64.
6. John Dewey, *Logic: The Theory of Inquiry* (New York: Henry Holt and Company, 1938), p. 156.
7. John Dewey, *Reconstruction in Philosophy* (New York: Henry Holt and Company, 1920), p. 169.
8. Ibid., p. 170.
9. Ibid., p. 175.

10. *Olmstead v. United States* 277 U.S. 438, 470 (1928).
11. 277 U.S. 438, 478.
12. *Mapp v. Ohio* 367 U.S. 643 (1961).

I

Bertrand Russell

The greater part of this chapter was abstracted from *Living Philosophies, Series of Intimate Credos* (New York: Simon and Schuster, 1931), Chapter II, pp. 9-19.

Nine sentences were taken from *The Philosophy of Bertrand Russell*, ed. P.A. Schilpp, Library of Living Philosophers (New York: Tudor Publishing Company, 1951). Reprinted *The Basic Writings of Bertrand Russell*, ed. Robert Egner and Lester E. Denonn (New York: Simon and Schuster, 1961), p. 38, 39.

Four sentences were taken from Bertrand Russell, *My Philosophical Development* (London: Allen and Unwin; New York: Simon and Schuster, 1959), Reprinted *The Basic Writings of Bertrand Russell*, ed. Robert Egner and Lester E. Denonn (New York: Simon and Schuster, 1961), p. 253, 254.

II

John Dewey

John Dewey, "From Absolutism to Experimentalism," in *Contemporary American Philosophy*, ed. George P. Adams and William P. Montague (New York: Macmillan and Company, 1930) Vol. II pp. 13-27.

III

Russell on Dewey's "Logic: The Theory of Inquiry"

Bertrand Russell, *A History of Western Philosophy* (New York: Simon and Schuster, 1945), p. 819.

The Philosophy of John Dewey, ed. Paul A. Schilpp, Library of Living Philosophers (New York: Tudor Publishing Company, Inc., 1939), pp. 137-156.

IV

Dewey's Reply to Russell

John Dewey, *The Quest for Certainty: A Study of the Relation of Knowledge and Action* (New York: Minton Balch & Company, 1929), p. 234.

The Philosophy of John Dewey, ed. Paul A. Schilpp, Library of Living Philosophers (New York: Tudor Publishing Company, Inc. 1939), p. 526 ff.

V

Russell's Rejoinder to Dewey

The Philosophy of John Dewey, ed. Paul A. Schilpp, Library of Living Philosophers (New York: Tudor Publishing Company, Inc. 1939), p. 571.

Bertrand Russell, *An Inquiry into Meaning and Truth* (New York: W.W. Norton, 1940), pp. 362, 401-410.

VI

Dewey's Rebuttal to Russell's
"An Inquiry into Meaning and Truth"

The Journal of Philosophy, Vol. XXXVIII. No. 7, March 27, 1941, 169-186.
Reprinted, John Dewey, *Problems of Men* (New York: Philosophical Library, Inc. 1946), p. 331 ff.

VII

Russell on Religion

Bertrand Russell, *Why I am Not A Christian* (New York: Simon and Schuster, 1957), p. 20, 22, 23, pp. 24 ff.

VIII

Dewey on Religion

John Dewey, *A Common Faith* (New Haven: Yale University Press, 1934), pp. 1-57.